Essays & Studies 1985

The English Association

The object of the English Association is to promote understanding and appreciation of the English language and its literature.

The Association is an international organization with branches at home and overseas. Its activities include sponsoring a number of publications and organizing annual sixth-form conferences.

Publications

The Year's Work in English Studies. An annual bibliographical survey of scholarly books and articles on English, American and Commonwealth Literature and Language. Published by John Murray (USA: Humanities Press).

Essays and Studies. An annual anthology of essays usually on a wide range of subjects from the medieval to the modern. A collector is nominated every year by the Association. Published by John Murray (USA: Humanities Press).

English. The journal of the Association, *English* is published three times a year by the Oxford University Press.

The Presidential Address. The Presidential Address, usually on a literary or linguistic subject, is published annually.

News-Letter. A *News-Letter* is issued three times a year giving information about forthcoming publications, conferences, and other activities.

Occasional Publications. The Association has published or sponsored many occasional works including *A Guide to Degree Courses in English* (Sixth Edition 1982), *English Grammar For Today*, *English Short Stories of Today*, *Poems of Today*, and many pamphlets.

Membership

There are three categories of membership. Full members receive copies of *The Year's Work in English Studies*, *Essays and Studies*, *English* (3 issues), three *News-Letters* and the Presidential Address.

Ordinary Members receive *English* (3 issues), three *News-Letters* and the Presidential Address.

Member Schools receive two copies of each issue of *English*, one copy of *Essays and Studies* (optional), three *News-Letters* and the Presidential Address. Schools Membership also offers preferential booking for Sixth Form Conference places.

For further details write to The Secretary, The English Association, 1 Priory Gardens, London W4 1TT.

Essays & Studies
1985

Collected by
Geoffrey Harlow

JOHN MURRAY, LONDON
HUMANITIES PRESS, ATLANTIC HIGHLANDS, N.J.

ESSAYS AND STUDIES 1985
IS VOLUME THIRTY-EIGHT IN THE NEW SERIES
OF ESSAYS AND STUDIES COLLECTED ON BEHALF OF
THE ENGLISH ASSOCIATION

First published 1985
by John Murray (Publishers) Ltd
50 Albemarle Street, London W1X 4BD

Typeset by Fakenham Photosetting Ltd, Fakenham, Norfolk
Printed and bound in Great Britain at
The Pitman Press, Bath

British Library Cataloguing in Publication Data

Essays and studies.—Vol. 38 (1985)
1. English literature—History and criticism
—Periodicals
I. Harlow, Geoffrey
820.9   PR1

ISBN 0–7195–4203–0

Humanities Press ISBN 0–391–03317–4

Contents

I

Sundry Ways of Love, Medieval Style

BEATRICE WHITE

Chaucer makes the point in *Troilus* that:

> Ek for to wynnen love in sondry ages,
> In sondry londes, sondry ben usages.

The wide field of human relations bristles with examples of 'sondry usages' in 'sondry londes', and with none more memorable than those of lovers.

Differences of time, place, and occupation in the context of human love can be well illustrated from two contrasting sources, the Inquisition Register of Jacques Fournier, Bishop of Pamiers (1318–25), and later Pope Benedict XII, concerned with unusual goings-on in a remote Pyrenean mountain village, Montaillou,[1] and English family papers of the fifteenth century.

Montaillou, enskied in the Pyrenees, was heavily infected with Catharism and the villagers, bookless but intelligent, were, many of them, heretics and interesting free-thinkers. It is their châtelaine, Béatrice de Planissoles, and her lovers who claim attention here. Béatrice was of noble birth and was married at an early age to the châtelain of Montaillou, Bérenger de Roquefort, in 1290. Permissiveness rather than promiscuity being the *modus vivendi* meant that, on the whole, wives were faithful (perhaps from fear of their husbands) and widows were often not. Béatrice's first affair was abortive. Her husband's steward, Raymond Roussel, a man of peasant stock, felt her attraction and suggested that they should elope to Lombardy. Béatrice was cautious: 'I am still young. If I go away with you, Raymond, tongues will start to wag. People will say that we have left the country to satisfy our lust.' Later they dined together and Raymond went secretly into the bedroom and hid under the bed.

---

[1] The material, preserved in Latin MS. 4030 in the Vatican Library, has been brilliantly interpreted and explored by Emmanuel Le Roy Ladurie, *Montaillou: village occitan de 1294 à 1324* (Gallimard, 1978); translated by Barbara Bray (Penguin Books, 1980).

'Then,' said Béatrice, 'I went to bed. Everyone in the house was asleep and so was I. Then Raymond came out from under the bed and got into it in his shirt. He made as if to sleep with me carnally. And I cried out, "What is happening?" Upon which Raymond said, "Shut up." To which I replied, "You peasant! (An insult)[2] Shut up, indeed!" And I started to cry out and call my servants who slept near me in other beds in my room, and I said, "There's a man in my bed." Whereupon Raymond emerged and left the room. A little while afterwards he left our service and went back to his own *ostal* in Prades.'

The second affair involved the Clergue family, the most important and wealthiest in the village. It was an illegitimate member of the clan, Pathau by name, who raped Béatrice while she was still a wife. As soon as her husband Bérenger died, she lived publicly as Pathau's mistress. He was succeeded as lover by his cousin, the parish priest, Pierre Clergue. This was a really serious affair, beginning in the confessional and continuing, literally, in the church. Pierre had only to declare, 'I prefer you to all the women in the world', for her to succumb to his embraces. She submitted herself to him completely, committing sacrilege, sleeping with him on Christmas night and in the church on a very dark night, where Pierre had installed a bed for them to make love on in the sanctuary of St Peter in Prades. 'Oh! Oh!' said Béatrice. 'How can we do such a thing in the church of St Peter?' To which her intrepid lover replied, 'Much harm it will do St Peter!'[3] The lovers were in the habit of meeting two or three times a week, and making love two or three times a night. While, according to local custom, she de-loused him, he would chat to her of social matters, of theology, and sometimes of contraception, a variety of which they practised. This affair lasted for two years, 1299–1301, and cemented a firm friendship. After the death of her husband, Béatrice was married for a second time, *c.* 1300, to Othon de Lagleise and moved from the mountains to the plains. There she met her lover who had come to her house under an assumed name, in the cellar, where beds jostled barrels. While her servant kept watch, Béatrice,

[2] Cf. the Viguier of Béziers to non-paying thirteenth-century peasants: 'O rustici sanguinolenti: vos dabitis, velitis vel non.'

[3] See the section on Penitence in *The Parson's Tale*, concerning confession by mouth of carnal sin committed in church. 'The chirche is entredited til it be reconsiled by the bysshop. And the preest sholde be enterdited that dide swich a vileynye; to terme of al his lif he sholde namoore synge masse, and if he dide, he sholde doon deedly synne at every time that he so songe masse.'

between the casks, 'mingled her body with that of the priest'. In 1308 when Béatrice was again a widow and seriously ill at Varilles, Pierre came to visit her for the last time. He sat on the bed, took her hand and stroked her arm. She told him she was worried about the heretical conversations they had held in the past and which she had not confessed. 'You have no need of confession,' she was assured, 'God alone can absolve sins.'

Widowhood could invite licence and at this stage Béatrice fell deeply in love with another priest, a much younger man, from a lower social stratum, and this time free from heretical leanings. His name was Barthélemy and in the fervour of her emotion, according to the young priest, she approached him directly. 'She threw herself at me,' he said and related that she invited him to her house when she was alone.

> I asked her: 'What do you want of me?' And she said, 'I love you. I want to sleep with you.'[4] And I answered, 'All right.' And straightway I made love to her in an antechamber and sub-sequently I possessed her often. But never at night. Always in the daytime when the house was empty.

To escape gossip the lovers moved to Palhars where they lived for a year before they parted. They were both subsequently imprisoned by the Inquisition, but released in 1322, Béatrice condemned to wear the double yellow cross of the heretic.

Perhaps the consciousness of the deepening shadow of the Inquisition and its perils helped to account for the recklessness that seems curiously desperate in attempting to snatch pleasure from danger, though, according to popular belief, there was no sin in pure pleasure.

Are we so very far here from a fictitious world where seductive lady and libidinous priest are familiar figures, playing laughter-provoking parts? Lovers abound in Fabliau and Romance, and we are prepared for whatever condign fate befalls them; but in the menacing world of fact it comes as an actual shock to realize that so vital, ubiquitous, and successful a lover as Pierre Clergue was to perish at last in the prisons of the future Pope Benedict XII, a victim not of love but of heresy.

Béatrice and Pierre, Raymond and Barthélemy, real people, aristocrat and villagers, lived in a remote, mountainous district. *Fine*

---

[4] For forthright ladies cf. Rimenhild in *King Horn* and Belisant in *Amis and Amiloun*.

amour had no place there. Nor had it a very obvious one among ordinary men and women domiciled in another country at a later time in a county, civic, and mercantile community, where commercial and practical issues were always paramount and where the excesses of lovers were generally controlled and mastered by cool sense rather than dictated by passion.

Chaucer's job in the Custom House as Comptroller of the London wool customs (1374–86) must have brought him into intimate contact with the prominent Merchant Staplers and Merchant Adventurers of his day. He, if anyone, was fully aware of the great importance of the wool trade to the country and the political significance of accumulated wealth. The wool trade and its powerfully influential wealth play an important part in the papers of four English families concerned mainly or partially with the trade in the troublous times of the Wars of the Roses—the Pastons, the Celys, the Plumptons, and the Stonors, who all flourished in the fifteenth century. Their family papers contain, amongst the more prosaic material, some unusual instances of romantic happenings.[5] 'Love', said Rutebeuf, meaning *fine amour*, 'is only for the rich', but a powerful sentiment, an 'elective affinity', an irresistible attraction, occasionally exerts its influence, making unexpected sallies into fifteenth-century merchant family circles.

Poets looking for frantic lovers could sometimes find them near at hand in a familiar, everyday, commercial environment, where they contrasted, not unpleasantly, with the more intense, intrepid Pyrenean lovers—noble lady and prurient priests—of an earlier time and entirely different circumstances, and, by their rare appearances, emphasized the firm pattern of English middle-class family life. There lies a mighty chasm of difference between the ebullient Pierre Clergue and Margaret Paston's domestic chaplain, the entirely respectable, trustworthy Sir James Gloys.

The Pastons were Norfolk folk, powerful landed gentry and prosperous merchants of the Staple who carefully chronicled all their affairs both domestic and mercantile. Sentiment rarely dictated their behaviour at a time when marriages were arranged as a matter of

[5] Editions of these letters and papers include: *Paston Letters and Papers of the Fifteenth Century*, ed. Norman Davis, Parts I and II (Oxford, 1971, 1976); *The Cely Letters 1472–1488*, ed. Alison Hanham, EETS 273 (Oxford, 1975); *The Plumpton Correspondence*, ed. Thomas Stapleton (Camden Society, 1839); *The Stonor Letters and Papers 1290–1483*, ed C.L. Kingsford (Camden Society, 1919).

business and partners were deliberately sought and valued for their potential wealth and worth in influence for the family. Parents were always on the lookout for suitable matches and relatives were always prepared to inspect the proposed candidate. This method of procuring mates did not entirely exclude personal preference. Sometimes brave obstinacy prevented a suggested match and often affection and loyalty graced an arranged marriage.

Within the family clan wives had a voice, powerful sometimes, but husbands were generally fully in control, 'servants in love and lords in marriage'. In the case of the Pastons the system of commercial marriages justified itself. Amongst the older Pastons, Agnes, née Berry, and her daughter-in-law Margaret, née Mautby, were formidable, courageous ladies who made devoted wives and careful mothers, demanding absolute obedience from their children. Agnes was described as 'a woman of virtuous living and disposition and of a good discretion and conscience'. Her daughter Elizabeth bravely resisted marriage with an ugly, diseased, elderly man and was, in consequence of her persistence, very harshly treated. A sympathetic cousin wrote asking for help (1449).

> She was never in so great sorrow as she is nowadays, for she may not speak to any man. . . . She hath since Easter the most part been beaten once in the week or twice, and sometimes twice in the day, and her head broke in two or three places.

It is, however, pleasant to record that the poor girl was subsequently married twice, first in 1459, and then again in 1472 to a very rich man, and so went up in the regard of the family.

The elder Sir John (d. 1479), Elizabeth's nephew, remained a bachelor after some unsuccessful philanderings. For a long time he was engaged to a court lady, Anne Haute, but the affair came to nothing. 'Bear yourself as lowly to the mother as you like, but to the maid not too lowly, nor that ye be too glad to speed, nor too sorry to fail' was his considered—if in his own case unsuccessful—advice to his brother. His sister, Margery, had a mind of her own and courageously refused to be deterred from her purpose of marrying the family factor, Richard Calle, to whom she had solemnly engaged herself in spite of family opposition. 'He should never have my goodwill to make my sister sell candle and mustard in Framlingham' was the fraternal verdict. Her mother was furious, refused to receive her and said, 'We have lost of her but a brethel'—a harsh dismissal. But

Margery persisted and was married to Richard Calle (1469) who subsequently became an important person in the county with a manor of his own.

Another brother, the second Sir John (the two had the same name), proved 'a crafty wooer', making very careful enquiries before venturing into matrimony, which he eventually did in 1477. The lady was Margery Brews, 'a witty gentlewoman, both good and virtuous' and certainly very charming as revealed in her letters. 'If,' she writes to Sir John, 'you could be content with that good [the proposed dowry] and my poor person, I would be the merriest maiden on ground.' He was her 'right reverent and worshipful and right well beloved Valentine', language which suggests a future successful marriage. Sir John II kept a wary eye on chances for his younger brother, writing to his mother, Margaret (1478),

> I heard while I was in London, where was a goodly young woman to marry, which was daughter to one Self, a mercer, and she shall have 200 l. in money to her marriage and 20 marks by year of land after the decease of a stepmother of hers which is upon fifty years of age and ere I departed out of London I spoke with some of the maid's friends and have gotten their good wills to have her married to my brother Edmund.

But Edmund eventually (1480) linked himself in matrimony with the rich widow Clippesby. The younger members of the family were certainly conscientious and strenuous in their search for moneyed wives. William Paston, still at Eton, didn't neglect his opportunities and requested his brother, John II, to look well at the proposed young lady's hands, 'for, as it is told me, she is disposed to be thick [plump]' (1479).

Amid the cold calculations of business arrangements the occasional love match sometimes meets with genial approval. In 1495 (?) Sir John Kendal, Prior of the Knights of St John, wrote to Sir John Paston II fully agreeing to the marriage of Constance, natural daughter of Sir John I, his elder brother, to John Clippesby, ward and stepson of Edmund Paston:

> At that time I knew not what love was betwixt them; but now I understand that both their minds are to marry together; whereunto on my part I am agreeable and well content, desiring and praying you to be the same and to be the better friend unto them at this my prayer and instance.

Such generous intercession deserved to be successful.

It is difficult to realize that these complicated business negotiations were taking place against a background of lawless violence, a background that in *Sir Degrevant* was sublimated into romance, fiction elaborating fact. In the midst of all the turbulence of economic change and social dislocation, and the diversion of the country's vital energies into new channels of trade and industry, the firm structure of family life remained unshaken. The bitter troubles of the time disrupted social life in country districts far less than might have been expected.

The Stonor family, of Stonor, some five miles from Henley, was, like that of the Pastons, composed of county gentlemen of great wealth, extensive estates, and a lively interest in the wool trade. Thomas Chaucer, the poet's son, was a family friend and they were acquainted with the Celys in the way of business. (Stonor fells were placed above the Celys' behind the mast of the *Thomas* of New Hythe.) In the summer of 1475 Elizabeth Ryche, widow of Thomas Ryche, a wealthy mercer, married William Stonor, and it was this marriage which promoted Stonor interest in the wool trade. Katharine Ryche, Elizabeth's young daughter by her first marriage, was courted by Thomas Betson, Stonor's partner, whom she married in 1478. On 1 June, 1476, Betson wrote a charming letter to his youthful betrothed from Calais where he worked at the Staple:

> If you would be a good eater of your meat always, that you might wax and grow fast to be a woman, you would make me the gladdest man of the world, by my troth. . . . Almighty Jesu make you a good woman, and send you many good years and long to live in health and virtue to his pleasure. At great Calais on this side of the sea, the first day of June, when every man was gone to his dinner and the clock struck nine, and all our household cried after me and badde me come down! Come down to dinner at once! And what answer I gave them you know it of old. By your faithful cousin and lover Thomas Betson.

Further references in the correspondence relate to the lady; one, in a letter to her mother, reveals Betson's tender concern for his young bride:

> I remember her full oft, God knows it. I dreamed once she was thirty winters of age: and when I woke I wished she had been but

twenty: and so by likelihood I am sooner like to have my wish
from my dream the which I beseech Almighty Jesu heartily may
be when it shall please him.

Betson died in 1486, and his wife, Katharine, married as her second
husband William Welbek, a haberdasher. She died in 1510, directing
that she should be buried by the side of her first husband at All
Hallows, Barking.

Between the years 1475 and 1479 Elizabeth Stonor plays a large
part in the correspondence of her family. She seems to have been a
very masterful woman. Her letters show her complete devotion to
her husband, but on her death in 1479, he ended his association with
mere citizens and prepared to improve his social position. This he did
by marrying in 1480 his second wife, Agnes Wydeslade, a very rich,
childless widow. She was said to have set her heart on him, writing to
him as 'Right worshipful master' and offering 'such service as I can
and may, thanking you of your kindness shown to me so poor a
woman as I am' and declaring herself 'Your true lover'. By May 1481
she was dead.

She was succeeded, not by a widow, but by a young girl nobly
born, Anne Neville, daughter of John, Marquis of Montagu, brother
of the Kingmaker. In February 1482 she wrote to Sir William Stonor:
'Sir, I recommend me unto you in my most hearty wise, right joyful
to hear of your health,' signing herself, 'Your new wife, Anne
Stonor'. She bore him two children and died in 1486. Sir William was
subsequently attainted but his estates, forfeited on his attainder, were
restored by Henry VII. The death of Anne ended his matrimonial
career and he remained a widower until he died in 1494.

While the Pastons in distant Norfolk had to defend their property
against the incursions of aggressive nobles, the Celys of Essex and of
London, and the Stonors of Oxfordshire had no such problems. The
Plumptons, who appear in both the Cely and the Stonor letters,
were, however, seriously incommoded by involvement in Northern
insurrections. They were a Yorkshire family from Plumpton, near
Knaresborough in the West Riding, coming early into history with
an account of a dramatic incident recorded by Roger of Hoveden. In
1184 Gilbert de Plumton was rescued from death by the timely
intervention of Baldwin, Bishop of Worcester, who came to his aid
when he stood, fettered and blindfolded at the gallows' foot, found
guilty and sentenced to be hung for the rape of Roger de Guilevast's
daughter. The sentence, subsequently annulled by the King, had

been enforced by the Justiciar, Ranulf de Glanvil, who had cherished other ideas for the disposal of the lady.

In 1472 the head of the family was Sir William Plumpton, a strange, insidious, unscrupulous man. In that year enquiry was made into the scandal caused by his deliberately keeping his second marriage secret. If there was any excuse for this it was, perhaps, to secure his estates to his son Robert, his two sons by his first wife, Elizabeth Stapleton, having died and left only daughters. The injustice done to his second wife, Jane Wintringham, is not easy to estimate at this distance in time, but it must have been considerable. However, Robert did his best to right the wrong done to her, though the painfully protracted lawsuit in which he became involved ruined him and reduced him to poverty. His letters reveal him as a thoroughly agreeable character whose relations with his wife, Agnes Gascoigne (d. 1504), suggest both deep affection and loyalty—'My dear heart' he calls her, and 'My right heartily and entirely beloved wife', and he signs himself 'Your own lover'. He died in 1523.

Pastons, Stonors, and Plumptons were primarily county gentlemen, though with serious interests in trade. But the Essex and London Celys were, first and foremost, very successful merchants of the Staple. Busy, rich tradesmen, they had the same attitude to marriage as their contemporaries—strictly practical, an aid in building up the family fortunes. As a result of a lawsuit their carefully preserved papers, both business and domestic, landed up in the Public Record Office and from them we can reconstruct their daily affairs.

Of the three sons active in the business, Robert was the black sheep. An inveterate gambler, he had, after the death in 1479 of his first wife, courted Jane Hart. He soon quarrelled with her and his father persuaded her to call the match off. She was allowed to keep 'a golden girdle, a little gold ring with a little diamond, and a damask tippet'. Later Robert left the wool business and became a fishmonger. By 1485 he was dead.

The two other brothers, Richard and George, were partners and ran the firm from Calais, London, and the Cotswolds. In 1481 they were both on the alert for suitable wives. On June 14th Richard wrote to George in Calais that he had met up with close friends, the Daltons, fellow Staplers, and reminded his brother how

We talked together in our bed of Dalton's sister. . . . I saw her and she was at breakfast with her mother and us. She is as goodly a young woman, as fair, as well-bodied and as sad as I see any this seven year. . . . I pray God that it may be imprinted in your mind to set your heart there.

There was no response to this. On May Day 1482 Richard was shown a most eligible young lady, an heiress, at Matins in North-leach Church. He shared wine and a roast heron with her and had 'right good communication'. But regardless of her merits the affair came to nothing. A little later a friend suggested as a possible bride Anne, daughter of Richard Rawson, a wealthy mercer from York-shire who became alderman and sheriff of London. She had a dowry of five hundred marks. This, if not the lady, made the grade, and the pair was married in February 1483.

According to Sir John Paston I, Calais was a 'merry town'. George, who ran that end of the Cely business, would have agreed. He certainly enjoyed himself learning to dance and to play musical instruments. He also tried his hand at poetry and became a wildly extravagant sportsman, to the despair of his brother and father. He kept mistresses as well. But in 1484 he settled down in holy mat-rimony with Margery Rygon, the widow of Edmond Rygon, rich citizen and draper of London, provoking by his lavish expenditure the protests of his sister-in-law. Margery proved a devoted wife, as her letter of 14 September suggests:

> Right reverend and worshipful Sir, I recommend me unto you with reverence, as a spouse ought to do to her spouse, as heartily as I can, evermore desiring to hear of your welfare the which Jesu preserve to His pleasure and your heart's desire. As soon as you may make an end of your business I pray you to speed you home, for I think it is a long season since you departed from me, and I wot well I shall never be merry till I see you.
> By your wife,
> Margery Cely.

If this letter suggests affection and devotion, what are we to make of this one, written on 26 May 1479: 'Très cher et especial, je me recommand à vous, Jorge Sely. Mon coeur n'est mis [sur] autre homme que sur vous, mais je pense que votre amour n'est point sur moy. Tout le coeur de Clare est à vous, Jorge Sely, toujours en mon coeur.' It was from one of his mistresses.

In the immense variety of medieval life official records and fam-iliar letters preserve a rich repository of human experience. They contain the raw material of which literature is made, impressively evidencing 'sondry usages' in 'sondry londes' 'to wynnen love'. The châtelaine of Montaillou and her lovers would be perfectly at their ease in any French fabliau or English Canterbury Tale. The practical Pastons and Celys and their merchant contemporaries, reluctant hosts to sentiment, occasionally found their comfortable business world and careful commercial marital arrangements utterly disrupted by the wanton and undeniable intrusion of a powerful emotion strong enough to rival the refinements of *fine amour*, an emotion both human and indestructible, quickly learnt, we are told, in gentle hearts and capable of moving the sun and the vast infinitude of the stars.

> The god of love, a, *benedicite*,
> How mighty and how greet a lord is he!

Chaucer was well aware of his considerable and capricious powers. Alison of Bath, a vigorous, independent character, regretted 'that ever love was sin'. The heretics of Montaillou would have laughed at such a notion and George Cely would have joined in the laughter. So would Bessy Bunting, the miller's daughter, and the Nut Brown Maid might have allowed herself a quiet chuckle. But let Dryden have the last word: 'Mankind is ever the same and nothing is lost out of Nature though everything is altered.'[6] In formal chronicles and family letters we have ample evidence to prove the abundant bounty of 'God's plenty'.

[6] Preface to *Fables, Ancient and Modern* (1699).

Feminine Response to Masculine Attractiveness in Middle English Literature

MARIE COLLINS

The Wife of Bath, whose mind should have been on more sombre matters during her fourth husband's funeral procession, was so strongly attracted by clerk Jankyn's 'clene and faire' legs and feet that she instantly committed her whole heart into his power.[1] Her case is however atypical of the examples with which this paper will mainly deal (leaving aside the overall grotesquerie of the situation): she is unusual in speaking with such precision of the parts of the body prompting strong physical attraction; she was no longer young (forty, in fact) when it happened; and she has little claim to be regarded as courtly. In considering the attributes inducing a favour-able response in well-born young women to desirable men, I have chosen the term 'attractiveness' on purpose to include, not only physical beauty, but also social and moral qualities: it will be the general contention of this paper that medieval heroines are usually shown responding to 'personability', the sum of abstract and con-crete qualities, rather than to mere handsomeness. I shall also try to show that the type and purpose of the deliberation applied by heroines to analysing their response and determining their conse-quent behaviour differ somewhat from the type and purpose of masculine meditation on feminine attractiveness.

That looks are by no means everything in medieval masculine portrayal was noted early this century by Walter Clyde Curry in a useful study:

> ... generally, in portrayals of manly beauty comparatively small space is given to the presentation of the personal appearance alone. On the other hand, the poet never tires of heaping up epithets in his attempts to delineate the noble and wise character of his hero and to show forth his manly virtues ... Tho this tendency to develop character at the expense of personal description is felt most strongly in the chronicles, yet it prevails also to a large extent

[1] F.N. Robinson, ed., *The Works of Geoffrey Chaucer* (2nd edition, London, 1957), pp. 81–2 (*The Wife of Bath's Prol.*, III (D) 593–602). All Chaucer quotations in this article are taken from Robinson's second edition.

in the romances as well ... Probably both the poet and his audience understand that, if the hero is young and of noble birth (as he almost always is), valiant, powerful, loyal and true, he is therefore necessarily handsome.[2]

Curry is speaking of general rather than specifically sexual attractiveness in masculine portrayal at this point, though many of the heroes he subsequently deals with prove attractive to women during their adventures. The question arises of whether women are depicted as responding favourably to a mixture of qualities, more abstract than concrete, in men, because this is felt to be peculiarly appropriate to the feminine disposition or station, or of whether they are shown reacting in this way because the conventions of masculine portrayal dictate that this mixture is simply what is available, in most literary works, for the heroine to respond to. There is evidence for both views, which are in any case not mutually exclusive.

Though the Middle English romances were hardly composed by poets anxiously clutching their style-manuals, they do not escape the influence (albeit at several removes) of classically-derived rhetorical practice. The comparative paucity of physical detail in the portrayal of personable young men reflects, however distantly, principles of masculine description derived by medieval theorists from classical sources. Although exterior description (*effictio*) and character-delineation by trait (*notatio*) had been clearly distinguished by theorists (such as the anonymous author of the *Rhetorica ad Herennium*[3]) from an early time, in practice it is commoner (except in the exemplary school-exercise) to combine elements of the two. Ernest Gallo, considering Geoffrey of Vinsauf's debt to his classical masters, points out that

> Both of these forms of Description employ certain commonplaces: in *De Inventione* (I.34–36) they are given as name, nature, manner of life, fortune, habit, feeling, interest, purpose, achievements, accidents, speech.[4]

[2] W.C. Curry, *The Middle English Ideal of Personal Beauty; as Found in the Metrical Romances, Chronicles and Legends of the XIII, XIV and XV Centuries* (Baltimore, 1916), pp. 4–5.

[3] Harry Caplan, ed. and transl., [*Cicero*] *ad C. Herennium De Ratione Dicendi (Rhetorica ad Herennium)* (London and Cambridge, Massachusetts, 1954), pp. 173–4, III.vi.10–11.

[4] Ernest A. Gallo, *The Poetria Nova and its Sources in Early Rhetorical Doctrine* (The Hague and Paris, 1971), p. 179.

As Gallo immediately goes on to indicate, the *Ad Herennium* (III.vi.10–11) lists the commonplaces of portraiture under three general headings, 'External Circumstances', 'Physical Attributes' and 'Qualities of Character'; he also quotes the later grammarian, Priscian, widely used in medieval schools, who similarly distinguishes broad categories of 'intrinsic' and 'extrinsic' attributes for the description of men (though the details differ from those of *Ad Herennium*). Classical epideictic rhetoric was geared to the twin purposes of praise and censure: medieval treatises, in inheriting its descriptive precepts, inherited advice about keeping the overall purpose and function of a portrait in mind and about selecting detail appropriate to the aim. Matthew of Vendôme says that physical description is relevant to the purpose in some cases and superfluous in others. He instances the fitness of character-delineation rather than physical description in Lucan's portrait of the austere Cato in the *Pharsalia*, to help the audience understand 'what follows about the heedlessness of Caesar and Cato's concern for liberty'. On the other hand, he indicates the need for physical description (here of a female figure) in a work treating sexual attraction, to prepare the audience to understand how the charms of Callisto caused Jupiter to burn with love for a mere mortal, which drove him to 'so vile an act' (here Matthew seems uneasily poised between aesthetic and ethical criteria of selection).[5] Later, on the subject of specifically masculine portrayal, Matthew makes an important general pronouncement. Still preserving the distinction between exterior description and character-delineation, he notes that male and female portraits require different approaches:

> . . . in praising a woman one should stress heavily her physical beauty. This is not the proper way to praise a man. As Ovid says:
>
> 'A nonchalance over physical beauty is becoming in man.'
> (Ars, I, 509)

In another place he puts it this way:

> 'A true man is concerned with his appearance
> Only within very moderate limits.'
> (Her., IV, 76) (Galyon, p. 46)

[5] Matthew of Vendôme, *The Art of Versification*, transl. Aubrey E. Galyon (Iowa State University Press, 1980), p. 34, §§38–40. For the Latin, see Edmond Faral, *Les Arts Poétiques du XIIe et du XIIIe Siècle* (Paris, 1924), pp. 118–19.

The underlying assumption of Matthew's adaptation of Ovid's famous pronouncements into literary *dicta* seems to be that the degree of attention devoted by an author to physical description of a man must reflect the extent of the subject's narcissism, whereas detailed description of a woman would not convict her of vanity. Both pronouncements have been considerably re-oriented from their original purposes: in the *Ars Amatoria*, Ovid offers disingenuous practical advice against dandyism to young men hoping to win women's favour, and in the *Heroides* it is Phaedra who makes the observation in praise of the stern masculine beauty of her stepson Hippolytus, whom she hopes to seduce. In Matthew, instead of indicating assumptions about female taste in masculine attractiveness, they are elevated, out of context, to the status of pronouncements on rhetorical decorum.

Though extensive physical description seems generally discouraged in the medieval masculine portrait, exceptions can be made for contextual reasons. Matthew of Vendôme concedes:

> Of course, sometimes a poet, to strengthen his case, describes the splendour of a young man's beauty as Statius did in his *Thebaid*, where he described the handsome Parthenopaeus as the very mirror of beauty. Statius emphasized this youth's beauty so that the reader might more easily understand the deep grief that even his enemies felt at his death. Statius calls him:
>
> 'The Arcadian whom both armies wept over equally.'
> (*Theb.*, XII, 807; Galyon, p. 47)

Geoffrey of Vinsauf deals with the fit choice of words for personal and other kinds of description (though not specifically with masculine portrayal at this point), suggesting the importance of tailoring the usual elements of description to the requirements of the whole context:

> If the subject is well set up, the whole work is polished. Keep an eye to the details and serve the tenor of the work; such detail suits prose as well as verse.
> (Gallo, p. 115)

The advice of both Matthew and Geoffrey takes into account the need to let circumstances alter cases, despite the normal practice of restraint in masculine description.

Turning from literary to amatory theory, we find support for the view that women respond to the personable rather than to the merely handsome man. Andreas Capellanus (who was not, as far as is known, directly influential in England, but who nevertheless stands in the Ovidian tradition available throughout Europe) discusses the five means by which love can be gained:

> a beautiful figure, excellence of character, extreme readiness of speech, great wealth, and the readiness with which one grants that which is sought. But we hold that love may be acquired only by the first three, and we think that the last two ought to be banished completely from Love's court...[6]

(The disputed degree of Andreas's ironic detachment need not trouble us here, since he claims merely to be reporting well-known 'teaching' about erotic attractiveness.) Andreas gives a surprising lack of emphasis to the first means of winning love, personal beauty—surprising because of the prominence given to the sight in his theory of falling in love, which forced him to deny the possibility of loving to people blind from birth.[7] For Andreas, personal beauty should be considered only to a moderate degree when one is attracted to a member of the opposite sex. Attractions based mainly on physical beauty are dismissed because love of this type can neither increase nor last, and brings only unhappiness; he considers the matter from the feminine as well as from the masculine viewpoint:

> A wise woman will therefore seek as a lover a man of praiseworthy character—not one who anoints himself all over like a woman or makes a rite of the care of the body, for it does not go with a masculine figure to adorn oneself in womanly fashion or to be devoted to the care of the body. It was people like this the admirable Ovid meant when he said,
>
> > Let young men who are decked out like women stay far away from me,
> > A manly form wants to be cared for within moderate limits.[8]

Andreas adapts Phaedra's words from the *Heroides* as tactical advice for male would-be lovers based on insight into female psychology,

---

[6] Andreas Capellanus, *The Art of Courtly Love*, transl. John Jay Parry (Columbia, 1941, reprinted New York, 1970), p. 33.

[7] Parry, p. 33.

[8] Parry, p. 34. Andreas refers to Ovid's *Heroides*, IV.75–6.

whereas Matthew of Vendôme's adaptation (see above, p. 14) turns them into a literary pronouncement based on concepts of decorum: both represent remarkable transformations.

Since looks are not everything, Andreas recommends excellence of character as the second of his ways to win love; it can even compensate for an ugly appearance (Parry, p. 35). His advice, he says, is for men and women alike, but once again he spells it out from the female viewpoint:

> If a wise woman selects as her lover a wise man, she can very easily keep her love hidden forever; she can teach a wise lover to be even wiser, and if he isn't so wise she can restrain him and make him careful. A woman, like a man, should not seek for beauty or care of the person or high birth, for 'beauty never pleases if it lacks goodness', and it is excellence of character alone which blesses a man with true nobility and makes him flourish in ruddy beauty.
>
> (Parry, p. 35)

Andreas then moves on to the third means of gaining love, readiness of speech, and the expectations of good character created by it:

> Many times fluency of speech will incline to love the hearts of those who do not love, for an elaborate line of talk on the part of the lover usually sets love's arrows a–flying and creates a presumption in favor of the excellent character of the speaker.
>
> (Parry, p. 35)

Much of Andreas's treatise from here on is devoted to exemplifying how men can play on female susceptibility with the gift of the gab, in the model conversations he gives. Andreas allows a far more important place to conventional rhetorical dexterity as a way of attracting women than does his classical mentor Ovid, who in the *Ars Amatoria* leaves sweet nothings to the lover's inspiration:

> Now is the time for talk with her ... Let not your eloquence submit to our poets' laws; see but that you make a start: your eloquence will come of itself. You must play the lover, and counterfeit heartache with words: her belief in that you must win by any device.[9]

[9] Ovid, *The Art of Love, and Other Poems*, transl. J.H. Mozley (London and Cambridge, Massachusetts, revised reprint, 1969), pp. 54 and 55 (*The Art of Love*, I. 609–12).

The Ovidian lover's attractiveness is assumed to be a product of the insincerity which permits artifice; for medieval heroines responding to masculine attractiveness, the problem is complicated by the need to distinguish the specious from the genuine, since at least the possibility is assumed that outward appearances may reflect true inner worth, hence the need for deliberation.

Before considering examples of situations where women respond to masculine attractiveness, it is worth looking at cautionary material depicting the pitfalls for women in that situation and offering caveats for their protection, for the insight it offers into medieval expectations about feminine reactions and behaviour. The Knight of La Tour-Landry, that conscientious father of daughters, retails his redoubtable late wife's dismissal of his enthusiasm for 'loue peramours': she charged their daughters 'that in this mater ye byleue not your fader',[10] cautioning them against the masculine wiles likely to win favourable feminine responses. Interestingly, she seemed more concerned about the dangers of persuasive verbal dexterity than about mere physical attractiveness:

> ... many gentylle men ... ben so fals and deceyuable, that they requyre euery gentylle woman that they may fynde; and to them they swere that they shalle kepe to them their feythe and be trewe to them, and shalle loue them without falshed or deceyuaunce, and that rather they shold deye than to thynke ony vylonye or dyshonoure, and that they shalle be the better preysed for the loue of them, and that, yf they haue ony good and worship, it shalle come by them. And thus they shalle shewe and saye to them so many reasons and abusions, that a grete meruaylle is to here hem speke. And yet more they gyue oute of theyr brestes grete and fayned syghes, and make as they were thynkynge and melancolyous, and after they cast a fals loke. And thenne the good and debonayr wymmen, that sene them, supposen that they be esprysed of trewe and feythfull loue.
>
> (*The Book of the Knight*, p. 175)

The true lover, by her account, is 'ferynge and dredefull', persuasive by his tongue-tied nervousness. Her scornfully reductive gallimaufry of the pleas and stratagems of would-be lovers receives its edge from her evident underlying fear that such tactics tend to attract young women. She would have found sympathetic the strictures of

[10] Thomas Wright, ed., *The Book of the Knight of La Tour-Landry*, EETS OS 33 (London, 1868), p. 172.

Gower's priest of Venus, Genius, about female susceptibility to masculine verbal and histrionic skills which make 'a woman wene/ To gon upon the faire grene,/ Whan that sche falleth in the Mir'.[11] Although the lesson in the *Confessio Amantis* is directed to a male hearer at these points, it contains standard cautionary material for women. The dangerous persuasiveness of the Ovidian lover, self-interested, self-controlled, histrionically skilled, intelligent and calculating, is illustrated by his medieval reflex, Chaucer's Diomede, who has a clear idea of what evokes a positive response from a woman, even to a man too rugged to be classically handsome (*Troilus and Criseyde*, V.799–805). He calculates his tactics, laying out 'hook and lyne' to 'fisshen' Criseyde (V.777): the results of his deliberation are apparent in his well-groomed appearance ('as fressh as braunche in May', V.844) at their second meeting, and more extensively in his verbal dexterity and histrionics. Just as his smooth tongue works cleverly round from generalities to his wish to be accepted as Criseyde's 'servant' in their first conversation (V.106–175), in their second (V.853–945) it similarly eases the progress from the general to the personal, allowing him to strike the appropriate attitudes—blushing, faltering speech, averted head, sudden silence, and an earnest glance (V.925–9)—with perfect timing. Criseyde's response will be discussed later; for the moment, we note how closely Diomede's calculated behaviour corresponds with that of the typical seducers feared by the Lady of La Tour-Landry for the success of their technique. Diomede's 'nothing venture, nothing gain' attitude is tellingly expressed ('I shal namore lesen but my speche', V.798) in that his 'speche' is his major, consciously-manipulated attraction, used to create 'a presumption in favor of the excellent character of the speaker' (Andreas Capellanus, translated by Parry: see above, p. 17).

The need for masculine attractiveness to be met with a degree of cautious deliberation by women is evidenced by treatments, mainly by Chaucer, of heroines brought to grief by an imprudent love. Laments by such women provide useful indications of what originally attracted them to their faithless lovers. Notably, manners, reputation, and especially a way with words figure larger than mere physical attractiveness. False speech and smooth tongues are promi-

[11] G.C. Macaulay, ed., *The English Works of John Gower*, I, EETS ES 81 (London, 1900), p. 54 (*Confessio Amantis*, I.681–3). The passage on hypocrite lovers is I.672–707.

nent in the laments: for example, in the *Romans of Partenay*,[12] the shape-shifter Melusine, when her husband has broken his vow and discovered that she spends her Saturdays in semi-serpentine form, utters an anaphoric 'catalogue'-lament of the qualities she regrets having been attracted by (lines 3578–95). These include his 'beute', 'ful gracious Aray', 'vertuous demenyng', 'werkyng amerous', 'gracious body gent' and his 'fals vntrew spech' and 'fals tonges unmesurabelnesse'. In Chaucer's *Squire's Tale*, the brokenhearted falcon laments her error of judgement in being attracted to her faithless tercelet (compared to the classic betrayer Jason) with revealing metaphors:

> So peynted he and kembde at point-devys
> As wel his wordes as his contenaunce.
>
> (*Squire's Tale*, V (F) 560–1)

Her error would have been avoidable had she first exercised the discernment implicit in the 'painting' and 'combing' metaphors indicative of the cosmetically-achieved artificiality of his attractiveness. Chaucer's *Legend of Good Women* provides almost a handbook of the dangers of an uncritical response to masculine attractiveness of the cultivated, Ovidian type. Once again, general 'personability' and a way with words seem to constitute the major attractions. Ariadne's heart, already softened with compassion by Theseus's imprisonment, is won by two elaborately courtly speeches (*Legend*, 2029–73 and 2103–22); his 'semely' (2074) twenty-three-year-old person may help matters, but her favourable smile is won by his 'stedefastnesse', 'hertely wordes', and 'chere' (2123–4). Phyllis, dazzled by the 'port and ... manere' (2453) of Theseus's son Demophoon, later laments putting too much trust into his 'lynage', 'fayre tonge', and 'teres falsly out yronge' (2526–7). Jason provides a comprehensive model of how to attract women, employing first retiring bashfulness with Hypsipyle and next elaborate eloquence with Medea. In the first instance, words nonetheless play an important part, reinforcing the effect of 'manere', 'aray', 'wordes', and 'chere' (1504–5) created at the queen's first encounter with the unknown Jason and Hercules: in the wooing, Hercules does all the talking (by pre-arrangement with Jason), recommending Jason's truth, wisdom, boldness, discretion, liberality, and pleasantness (1526–31), all qualities properly to be

[12] W.W. Skeat, ed., *The Romans of Partenay, or of Lusignan*, EETS OS 22 (London, 1866).

considered by a woman being wooed. Jason merely looks 'coy as is a mayde' (1548). Medea is attracted by the apparently ideal combination of qualities in Jason, handsomeness, lordly appearance, repute, regal glance, gracious, affable speech, and skill in love's art (1603–8). Her later lament for succumbing to an imprudent attraction is unusually specific about physical detail (though following the *Heroides* closely) in mentioning the beauty of his 'yelwe her' (1672) as well as the deceptive 'infynyt graciousnesse' of his tongue (1675). Dido is twice presented by Chaucer as a casualty of accepting a lover without proper deliberation, judging from appearances (and words) only. In *The Legend of Good Women* Aeneas's attractions are the complete 'package' (1066–74) of noble appearance, chivalry, strength, and verbal skill—'wel his wordes he besette can' (1069: cf. Gower, *Confessio Amantis*, IV.88–91, where the only attraction specified is his speech). The thudding, taggy rhyme conveying the charm succumbed to by Dido suggests the need for her more careful scrutiny (Aeneas 'hadde a noble visage for the nones,/ And formed wel of braunes and of bones', *Legend*, 1070–1). In *The House of Fame*, the narrator comments with commonsensical dismissiveness on her folly in being attracted by appearances and failing to deliberate; he speaks of her 'nyce lest,/ That loved al to sone a gest' (*House of Fame*, 287–8) on insufficient grounds, 'for chere,/ Or speche, or for frendly manere' (277–8). The narrator's attitude here carries Mrs Grundy's censorious tones, yet he is expressing a view about feminine response to masculine attractiveness stated as a principle by Andreas Capellanus, speaking of the four stages in love (giving hope, granting a kiss, enjoying an embrace, physical union): 'it is not seemly for wise women to give themselves so hastily to anyone, passing over the preliminary stages and jumping at once to the fourth ... because of the great thing that the yielding of her person is to a woman.' (Parry, p. 43.)

Turning now to examples of feminine response to masculine attractiveness, we find that they generally bear out what the 'cautionary' material showed in its different way, namely the importance of taking into account the whole person, not merely appearances and words, and the importance of cautious deliberation. Attraction by appearances only reflects badly on a woman's character: in *Sir Launfal*,[13] the pleasant but fallible hero, who becomes generally popular

---

[13] Text in Thomas C. Rumble, ed., *The Breton Lays in Middle English* (Detroit, 1965), pp. 3–43.

for his *largesse*, is seen leading the dance by the unpleasant queen Guinevere:

> 'I se,' sche seyde, 'daunce large Launfalle;
> To hym than wyll Y go.
>
> Of alle the knyghtes that Y se there,
> He ys the fayreste bachelere;
> He ne hadde never no wyf.'   (*Launfal*, 647–51)

True, Guinevere uses his epithet *large* ('generous, open-handed'), but without convincing us that she understands it in any deep sense as she precipitately decides to approach him ('Y love hym as my lyf!', 654). When an attraction is begun by appearances, trouble is taken to make the man's qualities reflect well on both parties. For example, in *Sir Degrevant*,[14] the sight of the hero attracts his enemy's daughter Melidor (467–72). His dazzlingly military appearance in gold, azure, and emblazoned armour conveys his 'borly and balde' (468) nature to her. Later, when he waylays her in an orchard at night, she is 'gretly affrayed' yet 'payed' for he is a 'comly knyghte' and 'ryally arrayede' (701–4); his appearance declares him a fit mate, even if she is too proud to admit the attraction yet. It is left to a lesser character, Melidor's maid and confidante, to give expression to Degrevant's sexual attractiveness: for the Christmas gift promised by her mistress, she says 'I aske noghte bot ȝone knyghte/ To slepe be my syde' (783–4). Much later, Melidor admits to Degrevant that for her it was love at first sight (1537–40), yet she retains the *mesure* to refuse Degrevant's request to anticipate their marriage (1530–6). The plot of the romance requires that Melidor, having been attracted by the hero, should be standoffish, not only because it is expected of a woman, but also on the practical grounds that she is falling in love with her father's enemy. The treatment of Degrevant's effect on Melidor creates convincing tensions between the erotic, moral, and social aspects of attraction, and emphasizes the worthy nature of both lovers.

Care to preserve the heroine from the imputation of dishonour is taken in depicting the process of attraction, especially when the woman acts to initiate an affair. In *King Horn*,[15] Rymenhild comes very close to discrediting herself when she summons the supposed

---

[14] L.F. Casson, ed., *The Romance of Sir Degrevant*, EETS OS 221 (London, 1949).

[15] Joseph Hall, ed., *King Horn* (Oxford, 1901).

Horn to her chamber and (in two of the three manuscripts of the romance) proceeds to 'wexe wild' (Cambridge MS, line 296; Harley MS, line 302). Counteracting any bad impression is the audience's knowledge that, since she has not spoken directly to Horn, she must have been attracted by the good qualities discerned by all who see him (and presumably emphasized by his recent programme of courtly education):

> In þe curt & vte
> & elles al abute
> Luuede men horn child,
> & mest him louede Rymenhild...
>
> (Cambridge MS, 245–8)

Inviting a young man in secret to a girl's room is imprudent, as the steward's anxiety shows, but at least Rymenhild has chosen a youth generally esteemed. A similar problem is similarly tersely dealt with in *Bevis of Hampton*,[16] where Josiane the heathen princess is the initiator of the relationship with Bevis. She falls in love with him, during his two-year stay amongst the heathens, for the same qualities which endear him to her father and the populace:

Beues was þer 3er and oþer	Beues was lovid with knyght
Þe king him louede also is broþer,	and kyng,
And þe maide, þat was so sli3:	For he was curtes in all thinge;
So dede eueri man, þat him si3.	Iosyan Beues can love
(Auchinleck, 577–80)	Ouer all erthly thinge above.
	(Chetham, 451–4)

The heathen king, not Josiane, comments on Bevis's beauty:

> 'Be mahoun, þat sit an hi3,
> A fairer child neuer i ne si3,
> Neiþer a lingþe ne on brade,
> Ne non, so faire limes hade!'
>
> (Auchinleck, 535–8)

Observations on a young man's physical beauty by a character other than the girl who falls in love with him preserve her unsullied by any taint of licentiousness; here it is particularly important to preserve our respect for the resourceful young infidel who will later

---

[16] Eugen Kölbing, ed., *The Romance of Sir Beues of Hamtoun*, EETS ES 46, 48, 65 (London, 1885, 1886, 1894).

make Bevis an excellent Christian wife. In the later Middle English rendering of *Partonope of Blois*,[17] we again find expression of the hero's beauty given to characters other than the heroine (again the initiator of the relationship with Partonope). Having fallen from the lady's favour, Partonope retreats to the Ardennes wild country, hoping for death, and loses his beauty and health. Eventually he is found accidentally by the lady's sister, who, with her cousin, nurses him back to health and his former splendour:

> When Wrak [the sister] be-helde a-boute right wisely
> His fressh coloure, his persone so semely,
> She ganne so nye fall with hym in dotage,
> Save þat wisdome restreyned corage...
> Persewyse [the cousin] stode in þe same degre...
> *(Partonope of Blois*, 7720–3, 7728)

In the immediate context, their susceptibility emphasizes the completeness of Partonope's recovery, but in the context of the whole it also convinces the audience that the lady's earlier unseen inspection of Partonope as a possible mate recommended by her envoys revealed physical as well as moral qualities highly pleasing to young women of royal or noble birth.

The need for cautious analysis before a woman accedes to an attraction is clear from the advice and tales of woe referred to earlier. When a young man is shot through the eye into the heart by Love's arrow, he does, it is true, indulge in extensive contemplation of the beloved, like Troilus, who makes 'a mirour of his mynde,/ In which he saugh al holly hire figure' (*Troilus and Criseyde*, I.365–6). It is not, however, the kind of thought on which decisions are based, or even the kind of thought which justifies or rationalizes a decision already unconsciously reached about a love-affair; it is, rather, the contemplation of adoration, analogous to religious meditation (Troilus and Palamon share a hyperbolic uncertainty about whether their beloveds are women or goddesses). It is indeed that 'excessive meditation' on the partner's beauty which gives rise to the 'certain inborn suffering' of Andreas Capellanus's definition of love (Parry, p. 28). For women, the thought about the partner's attractiveness comes at a different stage and for a different purpose. Ideally, it is a mixture of rational and moral analysis, determining, before

---

[17] A. Trampe Bödtker, ed., *The Middle-English Versions of Partonope of Blois*, EETS ES 109 (London, 1912).

commitment, whether the lover is worthy to be loved, or at least it is a meditation justifying the attraction on the basis of the man's good qualities. *Ipomedon A*[18] provides an example. When the Proud Maiden first sees the hero, the narrator gives a two-stanza portrait of Ipomedon, so overpoweringly attractive in red velvet, red silk, and ermine, that 'All hym lovyd, that lokyd hym one' (380). The Proud Maiden remains unmoved by this gorgeous manly vision: her expression remains unchanged, we are told, and her heart, well-established in wisdom, is as yet undaunted by love. Only when he has spoken with gracious yet humble courtesy does she waver inwardly; even then, she has time (and the self-command) to assess his potential status in the world's eyes ('she thought/ That he myghte with grette honoure/ Haue seruyd kynge or emperoure', 420–2), and her approach to commitment is slow and oblique ('A thynge in her hert gan ryse,/ That she shuld lyke wel hes seruyce...', 424–5). The world's assessment, actual or potential, of an attractive young man is important to the young woman weighing him up, often as a means of confirming her judgements by reference to external social and moral tenets. In the alliterative *William of Palerne*,[19] the princess Melior dwells at considerable length on William's qualities and the world's recognition of them (the place where she has set her heart is 'perles of alle puple... preised ouer alle' (499) and 'eche creature may know he was kome of gode' (504)). Once again, the particular requirements of the plot coincide with a common aspect of feminine behaviour when falling in love: William is a foundling, so Melior's interest in the general esteem for his noble qualities is in part to allay her own anxieties about a misalliance. In *Amis and Amiloun*,[20] the lady Belisaunt, the suitor of Amis, seems to need confirmation that her maidens discern in the hero all the qualities by which she is attracted, despite her boldness in other ways. In reply to Belisaunt's question, the maidens confirm boldness, beauty, and honourable appearance as the common opinion of Amis (448–68). Only then does Belisaunt give way to the attraction (it is a pity her later behaviour is not governed by comparable restraint, as it leads to a very painful chain of events for the friends of the title). In *Partonope of Blois*, in perhaps the most embarrassingly comic scene between lovers in medieval romance, the lady, the Queen of Byzantium, justifies herself to

[18] Eugen Kölbing, ed., *Ipomedon* (Breslau, 1889).
[19] W.W. Skeat, ed., *William of Palerne*, EETS ES 1 (London, 1867).
[20] MacEdward Leach, ed., *Amis and Amiloun*, EETS OS 203 (London, 1937).

Partonope for succumbing to him when they are in bed together (indeed, together anywhere) for the first time, using the unanimous reports she has received of his excellence to exculpate herself. In a tearful post-coital conversation, she stresses that the situation has arisen because her subjects were keen for her to marry. The envoys she sent out to inspect possible husbands brought back glowing reports of the nonpareil Partonope, esteemed by all:

> 'Off yowe they tolde so grette goodenesse,
> Off hey bewte so gret noblesse,
> Of curtesy so grette abondans,
> Þat þorowe alle þe remme of Fraunce
> Off gentylnes ye bere þe pryse,
> As off yowre age also ryghte wyse.
> Thys was proclaymed   þe hey renowne
> Off yowre manhode þorowe euery towne.'
>
> *(Partonope of Blois*, 1615–22)

These reports caused her to be shot by Love's fiery arrow through her *ear* into her heart, in a grotesque transformation of the usual metaphor for falling in love (1627–9). The general purpose of her speech seems to be to show Partonope that she thought about all the right things for a woman to consider in a man, and that the precipitancy of their mating does not mean she is a wanton:

> 'Where-fore, my loue, I yowe praye
> That ye neuer here-after þynke ne saye
> That I shulde euer to hasty bee
> To loue lyghtely, in no degre,
> To parforme any other hys plesyre,
> Alle-thowe I suffer yowre desyre.'
>
> (1677–82)

In more normal circumstances, deliberation and self-justification take place when a woman withdraws to think about a possible lover in solitude. In the prose romance *Valentine and Orson*,[21] the lady Clerimond, inspired 'ryght ardauntly' with love for Valentine, whom she has only just met, retires alone to the chamber where an oracular brass head is kept, and, on failing to get a satisfactory reply from it to her question about Valentine, thinks things over for herself:

[21] Arthur Dickson, ed., *Valentine and Orson*, EETS OS 204 (London, 1937).

When she had consydered by her self the maintene and the fayre speche and hardynes of Valentyne she was enbraced with his loue more than of ony other that euer she had sene and sayd Veray God what maye he be for aboue al lyuynge he is worthy to be loued, for he [is] pleasaunt 7 streyght, and of beaute corporall passing all other, and yf the heed of brasse do after my wyll, I shall neuer take other than hym.   (*Valentine and Orson*, ch. xxix, p. 135)

The most complex and interesting example of a woman who has retreated to her 'closet' to deliberate on a possible lover is provided by Chaucer's Criseyde (*Troilus and Criseyde*, II.598–812). When she first retires to 'wind up and down' what Pandarus has said, all she has to go on is his account of the love felt by 'the kynges deere sone,/ The goode, wise, worthi, fresshe, and free' (II.316–7) of whom she has hitherto held the same good opinion as she holds of her helper, his brother Hector (II.183–4). After the initial astonishment, her first thoughts are of how the situation affects her: she has nothing to fear because, no matter how much a man may love, a woman need not reciprocate unless she wishes (II.603–9). At this point her meditation is interrupted by the noise of the Mars-like victorious Troilus's return from battle past her house; she observes him, unknown to him, and 'al his chere' gently makes a profound impression on her heart, so that she asks herself 'Who yaf me drynke?' (II.651) (which, I take it, means something like 'Where does this sense of intoxication [with love] proceed from?'). Only then, when the spontaneous attraction has occurred, does she begin to deliberate in a manner comparable to Clerimond and the Proud Maiden, taking into account the whole person, Troilus's 'prowesse', 'wit', 'shap', 'gentilesse', and above all the flattering 'distresse' he feels for her (II.660–4), though she cannot yet consider one of the usual attractions, his words, as Pandarus has spoken for him so far. (When Troilus eventually does speak to her, he proves the Lady of La Tour-Landry's point that true lovers are incoherent or dumbstruck.) At this point comes the narrator's defence of Criseyde against the charge of 'sodeyn love' (II.667), in which he points to the gradual way in which love burrowed into her heart (II.673–9), a defence seen by critics as backhanded (though not always in the same way: see Ian Bishop's comments in *Chaucer's Troilus and Criseyde: a Critical Study*[22]). Ian Bishop takes the very fair view that 'what we should perhaps be worrying about is rather the evidence of her tardiness and

---

[22] Ian Bishop, *Chaucer's Troilus and Criseyde* (Bristol, 1981), p. 63.

equivocation' but that 'For the moment, however, she is genuinely
perturbed and confused by contrary impulses', even in the somewhat
formal subsequent monologue in which she turns things over in her
mind (Bishop, pp. 63–4). To view Criseyde's meditation in the light
of a conventional and proper part of a romance heroine's response to
masculine attractiveness (here coupled with an indirect proposal of
love) is to find some further grounds for the more charitable interpretation. Yet inevitably this is qualified by the amount of stress
given by Criseyde to her honour, reputation, and position and the
possible effect of a love-affair with a prince on these. As so often,
Chaucer here takes the materials of romance and subtly transmutes
them: to the 'set-piece' of the heroine's deliberations in response to a
man's attractions, he gives both genuine emotional force, in
Criseyde's perturbation, and a slightly tinny reverberation, in the
after-effect of her stress on self. That hollow ring is uncomfortably
recalled when we are given the much briefer account of how
Criseyde deliberates about taking another lover, the smooth
Diomede, whose tactics have already been commented on as calculated to succeed with women. She spends a night 'Retornyng in hire
soule ay up and down/The wordes of this sodeyn Diomede'
(V.1023–4). This time the influential factors are purely practical: 'His
gret estat, and perel of the town,/ And that she was allone and hadde
nede/ Of frendes help' (V.1025–7). The reason for her decision to
stay with the Greeks begins to 'brede' (V.1027) from this night's
deliberation. The spontaneous attraction which let us excuse her
slight self-centredness in considering Troilus as a lover is absent; her
night of thought about Diomede reads like a perfunctory parody of a
romance heroine's response to a lover's approach, for it lacks the vital
ingredient of appreciation either of his personal attractions or of his
qualities of character, and consists entirely of considerations of
Criseyde's welfare.

    In conclusion, for the women of medieval romance fiction,
response to masculine attractiveness is governed not so much by
personal beauty, for which a literary-historical reason has been
suggested, as by general 'personability', the sum of various moral
and social qualities, and by awareness that a certain amount of careful
thought must be devoted to the matter before commitment. Too
little deliberation produces a tearful Phyllis, too much a Criseyde
ignominiously 'rolled ... on many a tonge' (V.1061).[23]

[23] An earlier version of this paper was read to the International Courtly
Literature Society (British Branch) in Cambridge in January 1984.

III

The Image of the City in English Renaissance Drama[1]

WILLIAM TYDEMAN

Rapidly accelerating progress in British urban historiography during recent decades has considerably enhanced our understanding of the early modern civic community.[2] Indeed, for those whose researches into Renaissance drama are necessarily restricted to an all-too-finite collection of texts, the wealth of material at the Tudor historian's command can seem enviably extensive. Yet, by contrast with those seeking a deeper knowledge of sixteenth-century urban conditions, students of dramatic literature can do more than record those allusions to city life which Tudor plays occasionally vouchsafe in describing their location. On stage mere physical setting is often of less relevance than its contribution to a play's social, moral, or psychological significance:[3] drama exercised a novel influence over the way in which Renaissance audiences viewed their urban habitat, and the spirit in which they evaluated its ethos. It is therefore pertinent to analyse the stance drama adopted towards cities, and the manner in which plays presented it; to examine the impact on human behaviour and lifestyles which playwrights correctly or incorrectly attributed to urban factors; and most essentially, to consider the use of the civic image as a dramatic symbol. To assess the portrait of the city as it emerges from a study of English plays composed roughly between 1500 and 1600 may place in sharper relief, not merely urban conditions or contemporary reactions to them, but the theatrical treatment of a phenomenon of increasing economic, social, and ethical potency.

[1] This essay evolved from a paper presented to the Society for Renaissance Studies (Welsh Branch) at its biennial colloquium, November 1983.

[2] See, for example, *Crisis and Order in English Towns 1500–1700*, ed. Peter Clark and Peter Slack (London, 1972); *Perspectives in English Urban History*, ed. Alan Everitt (London, 1973); John Patten, *English Towns 1500–1700* (Folkestone and Hamden, Conn., 1978).

[3] See Raymond Williams, 'Social environment and theatrical environment; the case of English naturalism', in *English Drama: Forms and Development*, ed. Marie Axton and Raymond Williams (Cambridge, 1977), pp. 203–23.

Only by degrees does the city assume positive identity in English drama. Few early playwrights seem any more preoccupied with the implications of geographical locale than they do with chronological time. For this the tardy evolution of realistic scenery may be responsible, but clearly any concern to link character and environment in a naturalistically causal manner is only fitfully and unconsciously present. Not that the presentation of cities in early English plays relies on the direct transcription of actualities. In the medieval religious cycles, for instance, contextual considerations appear to inhibit those bold strokes by which biblical events are commonly assimilated to native settings. Hence, although the cycle plays feature both Bethlehem and Jerusalem, few exploit the spirit of place implicit in the scriptural accounts. A kind of theatrical functionalism rules, whereby Jerusalem, site of Christ's betrayal, Passion, and death, never acquires its own characteristic 'atmosphere'. Again, in Play XIV of the York Cycle, when Joseph complains of the crowds that throng Bethlehem's thoroughfares, indifferent to the plight of the Virgin and her unborn child, biblical data is expanded to convey information, not to point up the inherent symbolism of the situation:

> For we have sought both up and down
> Through diverse streets in this city,
> So mickle people are come to town
> That we can nowhere harboured be,
> There is slike press. . . . (lines 8–12)[4]

Only in one cyclic episode does the image of the city constitute a truly significant factor in the action. The author of *The Woman Taken in Adultery*, Play XXIV of the N-Town sequence, freely expands on an incident recorded in chapter eight of St John's Gospel, and so secures that climate of moral degeneracy and hypocritical self-righteousness informing the later delineation of urban society in the work of Jonson, Marston, Middleton, and Massinger. The efforts of sanctimonious Scribe and prurient Pharisee to compromise Christ with the harlot arrested while plying her trade exemplify the corruption of an environment corporately antagonistic to virtue, where sexual energy has been diverted inwards, and the guardians of public morals are more culpable than those who flout them. The savage hounding of the prostitute powerfully foreshadows Christ's own

[4] *York Mystery Plays: A Selection in Modern Spelling*, ed. Richard Beadle and Pamela M. King (Oxford, 1984).

fate at the hands of equally unctuous enemies, and this justly famous piece represents one of the few English plays of the Middle Ages in which the city becomes a vital ingredient in the anagogical pattern discernible from the dramatic totality.

The picture of the city conveyed in Renaissance drama must derive in part from medieval literary tradition, particularly that of satire and complaint.[5] Langland's *Piers Plowman* identifies urban communities with fraudulent conduct worthy of heavenly reprisal:

> Many sundry sorrows in cities fallen oft,
> Both through fire and flood and all for false people,
> That be-guilen good men and grieveth them wrongly...
> (C-text, IV.90–2)[6]

In particular, damage caused to the social fabric by the predatory tactics of administrators of the law is attributed to the civic establishment at Westminster: 'Westminster law, I wot well, worketh the contrary' (XI. 239). By the following century this gibe had become a literary commonplace, coupled with the notion that financial clout was imperative if one was to obtain legal satisfaction. The best-known poetic embodiment of the notion is the anonymous *London Lickpenny*, featuring a poor Kentish litigant, but Barclay's adaptation of Brant's *Narrenschiff* tells the same tale:

> Right many labours now with high diligence
> For to be lawyers the Commons to counsel.
> Thereby to be in honour had and in reverence
> But only they labour for their private avail.
> The purse of the client shall find him apparel
> And yet knows he neither law, good counsel, nor justice,
> But speaketh at adventure, as men throw the dice.
> (fol. xvi lines 8–14)[7]

The fifteenth-century morality *Wisdom* embraces a number of

---

[5] See John Peter, *Complaint and Satire in Early English Literature* (Oxford, 1956), and V.J. Scattergood, *Politics and Poetry in the Fifteenth Century* (London, 1971), to the former of which I owe several references cited here.

[6] Modernized from *The Vision of William concerning Piers the Plowman*, ed. Walter W. Skeat, 2 vols (Oxford, 1886).

[7] Modernized from Sebastian Brant, *The Shyp of Folys* (London, 1509), The English Experience, 229 (Amsterdam and Norwood, N.J., 1970).

prevalent attitudes to the city, laying particular stress on the perversion of justice, the frequent incidence of urban terrorism, and the sexual licence civic conditions permit. Mind, Will, and Understanding, all corrupted through Lucifer's agency, embody the worst aspects of the city's tainted lifestyle. Understanding summons to him 'the quest of Holborn', bribable jurors committed to perjury and malpractice, promising that the next term at Westminster will offer him rich pickings; Mind's threatening entourage includes allegorical aspects of sharp practice, while Will searches the 'lanes and ways' for sexual prey before resorting to the stews on Bankside. *Wisdom* offers the earliest evidence in English drama for the close association of moral degeneracy with urban opportunities.

But medieval tradition alone did not dictate the civic image in Renaissance dramatic writing. The influence exercised by the Roman comedies of Plautus and Terence offered imitators a conventional urban background rather more resonant than that derived from scripture by the cycle dramatists. Here was the familiar city street on to which open the house-doors of citizens and courtesans; to one side of the stage was assumed to lie the harbour with its shipping, while the market-place lay off to the other wing. From an environment which corresponded to those hackneyed townscapes known to us all from the Hollywood Western, the city acquired its comedic associations with intrigue and entanglement, amorous escapade and personal humiliation. When this legacy was passsed to Renaissance Europe, dramatists availed themselves of the opportunity to exploit this aspect of the city's stage potential. Such pieces as *Jack Juggler*, *Roister Doister*, and *The Comedy of Errors*, all of which are indebted to Plautus or Terence or both, depend in some measure on the classical portrait of the city as a *milieu* where stratagem and subterfuge thrive in their natural setting. Where medieval complaint literature warranted a stern admonitory tone, classical comedy sanctioned an indulgent smile.

At times, medieval and classical convention even coalesced in inculcating the view that communities such as cities and towns possessed the necessary machinery to ensure the resolution of conflicts and the righting of wrongs. As Raymond Williams points out in *The Country and the City*,[8] cities are 'centres of settled and often magnificent achievement' (p. 5), and a developed system of authority and control acts as a guarantee of order and stability in both private

[8] London, 1973.

and public affairs. Even Langland does not always despair of temporal justice, of

> Mayors and macers, they that ben mean [officers of justice,
> [intermediaries
> Between the king and the commons, to keep the laws,
> As to punish on pillories and on pining stools
> Brewers and bakers, butchers and cooks,
> For these are men of this mould that most harm worketh . . .
>
> (A-text, III.65–9)[9]

A number of Renaissance plays retain this image of the city as a force for social peace and harmony; by this means writers are able to present the urban community as one which not only contains the seeds of its own reformation, but exercises a positive influence for good.

The long-lived assumption that a moral chasm exists between a healthful, virtue-nurturing countryside and a pestiferous and corrupting city has been demonstrated to be nothing other than a myth.[10] Arguing that while greed and exploitation, crime and peculation, were just as rife in the country as in the town, Professor Williams demonstrates that a city environment merely made blatant economic and social processes which acquired spurious respectability in a pastoral setting. However, certain trends in early Tudor society arguably justified commentators in extending those anti-urban arguments already advanced in medieval writing. In some contexts cities came to be even more strongly associated with the evils of materialism, with social and economic selfishness, with conspicuous consumption and the miscarriage of justice, with the nurture of depravity and delinquency, with inhabitants who could contemplate extremes of poverty and wealth existing cheek by jowl without being moved to charitable compassion. Henry Brinklow, arguing from a Protestant standpoint, castigated London's 'inordinate rich stiffnecked Citizens' in 1545 in these terms:

> their heads are so given to seek their own particular wealths only,

---

[9] Modernized from *Piers Plowman: The A Version*, ed. George Kane (London, 1960).

[10] *The Country and the City*, pp. 46–9.

that they pass not of no honest provision for the poor, which thing
above all other infidelities, shall be our damnation ... I think in
my judgement, under heaven is not so little provision made for
the poor as in London, of so rich a City...[11]

His verdict is endorsed by Robert Crowley, who links hardness of
heart to self-seeking individualism on the part of officialdom:

> And this is a City
>   In name, but, in deed,
> It is a pack of people
>   That seek after meed;
> For Officers and all
>   Do seek their own gain,
> But for the wealth of the commons
>   Not one taketh pain.
> An hell without order,
>   I may it well call,
> Where every man is for himself,
> And no man for all.   (lines 193–204)[12]

Brinklow too has a keen eye for what he regards as 'the partiality
of judges, suppressing the poor, and aiding the rich for lucre, and in
condemning the innocents, and letting the wicked go free' (p. 92),
sentiments akin to those Thomas Starkey in his *Dialogue* placed in the
mouth of Reginald Pole:

> Judges and ministers of the law, you see how little regard, also,
> they have of good and true administration of justice. Lucre and
> affection ruleth all therein...[13]

Clearly such abuses were not confined to the city, but a later passage
in the *Dialogue* offers one explanation as to why injustice might be
adjudged a civic speciality:

[11] Modernized from Henry Brinklow, *The Lamentacyon of a Christen
Agaynst the Cytye of London, made by Roderigo Mors*, ed. J. Meadows Cowper,
EETS ES 22 (1874), pp. 79–80, 91.

[12] Modernized from Robert Crowley, *One and thyrtye Epigrammes* (1550)
in *The Select Works of Robert Crowley*, ed. J.M. Cowper, EETS ES 15 (1872),
p. 11.

[13] Thomas Starkey, *A Dialogue between Reginald Pole and Thomas Lupset*,
ed. Kathleen M. Burton (London, 1948), p. 86.

it is with us commonly used, that if any man have any controversy in the shire where he dwelleth, if he be purposed to vex his adversary he will by writ remove his cause to the court of Westminster—by the which mean oft-times the unjust cause prevaileth ... so justice is oppressed, truth overthrown, and wrong taketh place.   (p. 112)

The point is conveniently illustrated in one of Understanding's speeches in *Wisdom* in which Will is advised to have his rival in love bound over to keep the peace,

> Then in another shire him indict,
>   He ne shall weet by whom ne how.
> Have him in the Marshalsea seen aright...
>   (lines 851–3)[14]

Thus we have criminality, acquisitiveness, venality, sexual immorality, all featuring in the moral interludes of the early Tudor period as distinguishing trademarks of town life, whatever the literal state of affairs in country districts, which were certainly not unblemished or idyllic. However, rustics are often cast in the role of ingenuous dupes of their city cousins, who people a more sophisticated world.

Whereas in the fifteenth-century morality *Mankind* the Vice characters are not associated with urban activities, in the Tudor interludes they frequently have positive city affiliations. Skelton's *Magnificence*, though primarily a work of court provenance, characterizes the disreputable clique who bring the eponymous hero to the brink of disaster as frequenters of low taverns and the Bankside brothels. Folly, the engagingly amoral hit-man who enlivens *Mundus et Infans*, announces his abode as London, his place of upbringing as Holborn, and his training-school as Westminster where he served the law by fleecing poor men from the country seeking legal redress. His pastimes include frequenting taverns, at one of which he lives with his mistress, a 'fair tapster', satisfying any additional sexual needs over London Bridge at the Bankside stews. He prevails on Manhood, his intended victim,

> In Eastcheap for to dine:
> And then we will with Lombards at passage play,   [dice
> And at The Pope's Head sweet wine assay   (lines 671–3)[15]

[14] Modernized from *The Macro Plays*, ed. Mark Eccles, EETS 262 (1969). The court of the Marshalsea had a reputation for unfair practice.
[15] See *Three Late Medieval Morality Plays*, ed. G.A. Lester (London, 1981).

but far from learning 'revel', Manhood returns from London an aged man, his money lost through gambling, and his health broken by a spell in Newgate. The city is here unequivocally linked with those personal habits that bring men to near-ruination.

The Interlude of Youth is less steeped in urban allusions, though again one of the chief Vices, Riot, is characterized as newly released from Newgate, having been invited, according to his own claim, 'to preach at Tyburn' by the Lord Mayor himself, but having contrived to escape when the hangman's rope broke, much as New Guise eludes the gallows in *Mankind*. However, the city is not selected as the site for drinking and whoring, although when the figure of Humility appears, Youth enquires if he be a countryman or no:

> Were thou born in Trumpington
> And brought up at Hogs Norton?   (lines 603–4)[16]

Ian Lancashire may be right in attributing this gibe to university wit; this certainly seems to be the earliest allusion in English drama to what developed into the stock association of virtuous meekness with a pastoral *milieu*, and worldly-wise viciousness with the city. The same contrast informs the central scenes of Udall's *Respublica*, when the rustic People is insulted by the trio of Vices who defraud the widow Respublica of her rightful dues.

Hick Scorner too capitalizes on London's connections with vice and corruption. Here the Vice, Free Will, resembles Folly in frequenting inns and brothels, while Imagination, another agent of temptation, is linked with shady transactions in Westminster Hall and plies his trade in Holborn. Newgate and Tyburn again feature in the text. But now an element of gratuitous urban thuggery appears: Imagination encourages the Vices to seek a likely victim to rob:

> And if we meet a true man, make him stand,
> Or else that he bear a stripe.
> If that he struggle and make any work,   [cause trouble
> Lightly strike him to the heart
> And throw him into Thames quite.   (lines 414–18)[17]

---

[16] See *Two Tudor Interludes The Interlude of Youth* and *Hick Scorner*, ed. Ian Lancashire (Manchester and Baltimore, 1980).
[17] *Ibid.*

This notion of the city as the home of deceit and trickery persists into the middle and later decades of the century. One of the least didactic of plays to uphold this image is *Jack Juggler* where the befogging of the wits of the lackey Jenkin Careaway by his aggressive double is carried off with style, but motivated by little more than Jack's desire to make sport, while Jenkin's hints as to his master's sexual infidelities may owe something to Plautine convention. In *Impatient Poverty*, the victimization of the virtuous hero is made the basis for an approach much more anti-mercantilist and anti-judicial. Abundance, the principal agent of deception, who makes his living by lending at profitable rates, protests that

> this is no sin:
> It is plain buying and selling;
> Lawful it is for a man to win,
> Else rich shall he never be.[18]

Conscience responds that 'One such is able to destroy a city', but it does not move Abundance who cannot envisage how men can thrive in a commercial environment without the use of 'usury, deceit, and extortion', and certainly sees no necessity to restore what he has accumulated through trickery. The other major figure of interest, Colhazard, a *nouveau riche* gambler who

> came late from beyond the sea
> Ragged and torn, in a garded coat;   [ornamented
> And in his purse, never a groat;
> And now he goeth like a lord!   (pp. 336–7)

involves himself in a plan to reduce Prosperity (formerly Impatient Poverty) to his state of former wretchedness, by fleecing him of his fortune at dice and cards. Colhazard manifestly represents the contemporary spirit of economic opportunism; the more traditional mistrust of the judicial system is demonstrated later. While Prosperity is cast into the Marshalsea Prison for debt as a result of Colhazard's depredations, Abundance, faced with a charge of adultery, is astute enough to utilize his financial assets to buy off the law. The city maintains its reputation for corrupting the innocent and rewarding the affluent and unscrupulous.

Not that the law is invariably shown to be vulnerable to manipulation: *Respublica* depicts justice ultimately triumphant in the person of

---

[18] See *'Lost' Tudor Plays with some others*, ed. John S. Farmer (London, 1907; rept., Guildford, 1966), p. 323.

Nemesis, and in *Cambises* the venal conduct of Sisamnes in taking bribes and denying the poor justice is detected and punished. In *Appius and Virginia* the traditional tale of the dishonourable judge sees him commit suicide in prison, while in *Damon and Pithias* Dionysius, whose tyranny is reflected both in a pitiless legal system which shows the two friends no mercy and in the sharp practice of the palace collier and the palace porters, finally abandons it, inspired by the mutual devotion of the central characters.

In several social moralities of the 1560s and 70s the conclusion is optimistic, though civic corruption is made real enough. In *Enough Is As Good As A Feast* vice is once again given an urban face: covetousness occupies the seats of justice, avarice keeps prices high and sanctions the exploitation of those of slender means, the oppressed tenantry have difficulty in obtaining redress. Admittedly, Worldly Man, who put 'his money to usury', indulged his sensual appetites, and defrauded the poor, is carried off by Satan, but the rural tenant, shown as an old man from the Cotswolds, is seen seeking relief in vain from Covetousness, the steward. If rack-renting is the target here, in *Like Will to Like* unfair trading is the butt, the finger being pointed once more at a dishonest collier, although to him a rural idiom rather than a city one is assigned. However, of the urban origins of Cutpurse and Pickpurse, companions to Nichol Newfangle the Vice, there is no doubt. In this piece the Vice appears to be anxious to ensnare the vicious rather than the virtuous: his prime target is the formerly prosperous Roister and Tosspot, representatives of riotous living, but he ultimately secures the execution of Cutpurse and Pickpurse, his former colleagues in crime. *All for Money* is another vehicle for inveighing against avarice, although the operation of that cardinal sin is not regarded as resident in towns alone; All for Money himself is identified with the crooked magistrate of tradition.

In *The Tide Tarrieth No Man* the social consequences of urban corruption are set against a background of moral philosophy, the Prologue declaring that

So many cities and towns are defamed
By reason that some inhabitant is ill,
So that for one's fact the whole town is blamed   [evil deed, crime
Although the residue to good do their will.   (*Prologue*, lines 8–10)[19]

[19] See *English Morality Plays and Moral Interludes*, ed. Edgar T. Schell and J.D. Shuchter (New York, 1969).

Greed is once more seen as the besetting sin of the city-dweller, whether it takes the form of usury or the picking of pockets; one of the Vices, Feigned Furtherance, is a merchant's man. What plot there is turns on the devices of Greediness and others to bring men to disastrous ends, financial ruin temporarily having replaced spiritual annihilation as the ultimate human disaster. The optimistic conclusion brings on the figures of Faithful Friend and Christian to establish order, and Authority arrives in time to administer even-handed justice. Correction drags off to gaol the leading Vice, Courage (Cheek or Sauce in today's idiom), and the true stature of a city is pronounced to reside not in its splendid buildings and monuments, but in the moral virtue of its inhabitants:

> For to Socrates' saying some respect we have,
> Who saith a city is not to be praised
> For the greatness of buildings, gorgeous and brave,
> But for the good inhabitants which therein are placed.
>
> (lines 1741–4)

The picture is an encouraging one; the *status quo* is holding firm.

Few such feelings survive after the dispensation of justice at the close of that often-underrated masterpiece of Tudor drama, *Arden of Faversham*, in which the role assigned to London is of great significance. *Arden* is alive with all the social tensions of the late Elizabethan era, among them the fact that Arden is a newly-enriched gentleman while his wife's lover Mosbie is steward to Lord Clifford. It is almost as if Jack Juggler were now in a position to cuckold Master Bongrace! The taint of covetousness is no longer embodied in abstract personifications: Arden himself is shown to be miserly, a cold calculator who does not hesitate to enrich himself further by the legitimate and illegitimate appropriation of land. The acquisitive stain infects all classes: Arden's servingman, Michael, is prepared to murder his own brother to obtain his farm, and the hired assassins enter the plot through their connection with Bradshaw, grocer turned goldsmith, who seeks information on a thief with stolen property to dispose of. The message of the social moralities is here expressed by means of a 'human story' and functions within a recognizably local and topical framework. But unlike the morality world, Arden's has no authoritative representative of idealized virtue, justice, or repentance to take the role of a *deus ex machina* and ensure that the good end happily and the bad unhappily. The Mayor of Faversham is too weak a figure, dramatically speaking, to play the role of Nemesis with any conviction.

In no other Elizabethan play does the capital assume such an anarchic and sinister aspect: its contamination pollutes the tone of private and public life. Alice claims that her husband is keeping whores in town, and whether this is a falsehood or not, it is a tribute to the author's neutral stance that the charge does not seem totally fantastic. The hired thugs, Black Will and Shakebag, exude that spirit of mindless, conscienceless amorality already associated with London in the moralities. The presentation of the capital itself offers a portrait of a violent, lawless, and hostile environment where only the fittest can survive. This is nowhere more vividly conveyed than in Black Will's bragging speech in Scene XIV:

> I have lived in London this twelve years, where I have made some go upon wooden legs for taking the wall on me; divers with silver noses for saying, 'There goes Black Will.' I have cracked as many blades as thou hast done nuts . . . The bawdy-houses have paid me tribute; there durst not a whore set up unless she have agreed with me first for op'ning her shop windows. For a cross word of a tapster I have pierced one barrel after another with my dagger and held him by the ears till all his beer hath run out. In Thames Street a brewer's cart was like to have run over me; I made no more ado, but went to the clerk and cut all the notches off his tallies and beat them about his head. I and my company have taken the constable from his watch and carried him about the fields on a coltstaff. I have broken a sergeant's head with his own mace, and bailed whom I list with my sword and buckler. All the tenpenny ale-houses would stand every morning with a quart pot in their hand, saying, 'Will it please your worship drink?' He that had not done so had been sure to have had his sign pulled down and his lattice borne away the next night . . .   (lines 5–27)[20]

This could scarcely be bettered as a dramatic presentation of a community where anarchy rules and law and order are themselves powerless against the ruthless antipathy of those whose criminal activities reflect the grasping materialism of the world they infect. Even the observation of poetic justice is accompanied by cruelty and violence: Mosbie and his sister are executed at Smithfield and Alice

[20] See *The Tragedy of Master Arden of Faversham*, ed. M.L. Wine (London, 1973).

burnt to death in Canterbury; Shakebag murders the widow who refuses him sanctuary in Southwark, and is then killed equally casually himself *en route* for Greenwich; Black Will is 'burnt in Flushing on a stage'. In such a *milieu* there is no place for rejoicing over the repentant sinner.

However, it would be false to suggest that the city is universally presented in a pejorative light throughout English Renaissance drama. Medwall's *Fulgens and Lucrece* depicts the senators of Rome as capable of nice discriminations and sound judgement. Rivalry between the patrician and the plebeian for the hand of Lucrece evolves into a struggle for prestige in the eyes of the Roman citizenry to whom Publius Cornelius and Gaius Flaminius appeal by citing their services to the city. The inference is clearly that the good opinion of urban society is worth courting, especially in a matter where the ancient regime is in competition with the New Men of Henry VII's England, and Medwall's faith in the value of civic arbitration is in marked contrast to the morality playwright's dismissal of the city as the home of vicious conduct and fraudulent practices.

Almost one hundred years later, John Stow in his *Survey of London* (1598) accords the city high status for its public-spiritedness, its traditions of loyal service, its reputation for the defence of the realm, its maintenance of law and good discipline, its charitable works, in a discourse which defends the capital against the opinions of those 'which think that the greatness of that City standeth not with the profit and security of this realm'.[21] Stow rejects the notion that cities make for lawlessness—'men by this nearness of conversation are withdrawn from barbarous feritie and force to a certain mildness of manners, and to humanity and justice' (p. 483)—and his arguments are echoed in a number of plays. The anonymous author of *The Life and Death of Jack Straw* is at pains to show the citizens of London firmly aligning themselves with the king and the English nobility to suppress the Peasants' Revolt of 1381. The Kentish rebels, rustics to a man—'Tilers, thatchers, millers, and such like'—are provided with no justification for their uprising, but are presented in a critically satirical light, so that their destruction of the symbols of regal dignity and civic authority can appear more wantonly irresponsible. The indubitable hero is Walworth, the Lord Mayor, who in despatching

---

[21] See *Stow's Survey of London*, intro. by H.B. Wheatley, Everyman Library edn. (London, 1912; revd. edn. 1956), pp. 482–97.

Jack Straw personally, invokes the spirit of ancient Rome, his deed being thus deemed as worthy to rank alongside those who made 'old Rome' 'flourish for virtue, and for arms'.[22] The combination of the ancient Roman spirit, the city of London, God, Richard II, and the Lord Mayor, are reckoned to be a sufficiently formidable combination to defeat any rebellion, especially among the lower orders. The hallowing of the alliance between crown and capital is symbolized by the king's decree that from henceforth the mayor's bloody dagger shall be incorporated into the civic coat of arms.

Jack Straw is a bold, unsubtle play. Not so Thomas Dekker's masterpiece *The Shoemakers' Holiday*, which forms the apotheosis of a genre in which the idealistic portrayal of the *bourgeoisie* was given pride of place, a feature which Francis Beaumont was not slow to satirize in *The Knight of the Burning Pestle*. Dekker's play represents an overwhelming vote of confidence in London, its lifestyle, its moral code, its respectability, its positively benevolent tendency to encourage its citizens to good works and good behaviour. It is also a vote of confidence in the benefits of capitalism. Simon Eyre, the energetic and ebullient shoemaker, who rises from the workbench to become Lord Mayor, is the epitome of the model London entrepreneur: honest employer and loyal citizen, as fond of a prank as a party, bluff, kindly, generous, and ardently attached to his family, friends, workmen, trade, and city. His rise to wealth and civic distinction is not undermined by any of those dubious pieces of sharp practice or ambitious thrusting which one notes in similar figures in the moral interludes or in Arden, even if Dekker was forced to adapt his source in order to protect his protagonist's immaculate reputation.[23] Eyre's genial attitude to his workforce strains our sense of the credible at times, yet the tendency of the play is to make us accept his willingness to share his good fortune with others, his granting of a Shrove Tuesday holiday, and his institution of an annual feast for shoemakers' apprentices. The portraiture is equally idealized in the romantic portion of the action where this avuncular hero fosters the match between Rose, daughter of his predecessor as Lord Mayor, and the nobly-born Rowland Lacy. Eyre's role here vindicates the prestige of the city in the play: not only can the self-made businessman hold his own in the best of company, but the union

[22] Modernized from *The Life and Death of Jacke Straw* ... (1593), Tudor Facsimile Texts, ed. John S. Farmer, n.d., sig E2 recto, line 2.

[23] See Alexander Leggatt, *Citizen Comedy in the Age of Shakespeare* (Toronto and Buffalo, 1973), p. 18.

between an aristocrat and the daughter of a merchant is sanctioned by the *beau ideal* of the Elizabethans, Henry V.

Not that every dramatic accolade bestowed on London demonstrates the same tactful skill that Dekker brings to bear on his real-life fairy-story. Heywood's *Four Prentices of London* is the most extravagant example of a genre which exalted the prowess of the city's denizens for their own delectation. Only Heywood's supreme lack of self-consciousness could have led him to convert the legendary Christian champion, Geoffroi de Bouillon, one of the participants in the First Crusade, and his three brothers into London apprentices before sending them off on a series of chivalric adventures. The author's awkwardness in assimilating his hero into his mercantile setting is hardly surprising, however he may rationalize it:

> I praise that City which made princes tradesmen...
> I hold it no disparage to my birth,
> Though I be born an earl, to have the skill
> And the full knowledge of the mercer's trade...
>   (I.1.67, 73–5)[24]

A medieval nobleman need feel no shame in having an alternative career at his finger-tips, agrees his brother Guy:

> Say I be born a prince, and be cast down
> By some sinister chance, or fortune's frown;
> Say I be banished: when I have a trade,
> And in myself a means to purchase wealth,
> Though my state waste, and tow'ring honours fall,
> That still stays with me in the extrem'st of all.   (I.1.84–9)

The pragmatic bourgeois philosophy of resourcefulness receives further aristocratic endorsement when the brothers proceed to do battle with the pagan hoards under ensigns which bear the arms of the city companies. *The Four Prentices* may be felt to carry the doctrine of commercial self-reliance to the *ne plus ultra* of caricature, but held aloft by Thomas Heywood the image of the city is no longer a tarnished one. Arguably, however, the note of smug complacency in such dramas not only led Beaumont to mock the tastes and pretensions of the citizen and his wife in *The Knight of the Burning*

---

[24] Modernized from Thomas Heywood, *The Four Prentices of London*, ed. Mary Ann Weber Gasior (New York and London, 1980).

Pestle, but provoked dramatists of the new century to attack the covetousness and depravity of London merchants and usurers, lawyers and aldermen, with the same vehemence and bitterness displayed by those who had castigated the city as a place of iniquity and inequity over the preceding hundred years.

IV

Cowper's Olney Hymns

J.R. WATSON

Cowper's share in the *Olney Hymns* of 1779 has received less attention than the remainder of his poetry. This is partly because of a
prejudice against hymns, those 'quatrains shovelled out four-square'
as Robert Lowell described them,[1] which led early critics such as
Goldwin Smith into a brusque and sweeping dismissal ('Cowper's
Olney Hymns have not any serious value as poetry. Hymns rarely
have.'[2]); and even if we reject this as unconsidered and intemperate,
there is linked with it the suggestion that the composition of the
hymns was a duty imposed upon Cowper by Newton rather than a
poetic pleasure. 'Cowper', says David Cecil, 'dutifully carried out his
part of the bleak task.'[3] A glance at the hymns which Cowper wrote
should convince any fair-minded reader that their composition was
anything but a bleak task: that it was rather a matter of joy, following
the examples of Watts and Charles Wesley. But there remains the
suggestion that the hymns are, somehow, not quite central to
Cowper. So Patricia Meyer Spacks writes:

> What is particularly striking about Cowper's hymns as compared
> with his other work is their essentially slight dependence on
> imagery: their strength derives almost entirely from the quality of
> their psychological insight, and their attempts to translate that
> insight into images are rarely and incompletely successful.[4]

Vincent Newey, on the other hand, sees the hymns as all too central.
In his fine book, *Cowper's Poetry*, he sees the hymns as evidence that
Cowper was fundamentally anxious, uncomfortable, helpless,
imprisoned: 'What his hymns most powerfully realize is not so much

[1] Robert Lowell, 'Waking Early Sunday Morning'.
[2] Goldwin Smith, *Cowper* (London, 1902), p. 42.
[3] David Cecil, *The Stricken Deer* (London, 1929), p. 141.
[4] Patricia Meyer Spacks, *The Poetry of Vision* (Cambridge, Mass., 1967), p.
165. See also Lowick Hartley, 'The Worm and the Thorn: A Study of
Cowper's *Olney Hymns*', *The Journal of Religion*, XXIX (1949), pp. 220–9,
and Maurice J. Quinlan, 'Cowper's Imagery', *JEGP*, XLVII (1948), pp.
276–85.

even a "struggle for faith", but the struggles of a mind for which assured faith, and the repose that goes with it, are impossible.'[5] Newey's main argument is that 'Cowper's true convincing voice is to be found, almost without exception, in expressions of longing, uncertainty, desperation, weakness.'[6] A corollary of this is that when Cowper tries to celebrate the joys of religion (as in 'I will praise the Lord', the last of his hymns in the collection) his emblematizing, in Newey's words, 'could hardly be flatter' and there is a consistent 'inability to be inspired in the presence of the Saviour'.[7]

In this section, as elsewhere, Newey writes with great sensitivity: he sees the outward strength of the hymns, but also a spiritual unease that exists beneath, a certain doubt which adds complexity to the hymn form's undoubted robustness. Even 'God moves in a mysterious way' is seen as having its ironic undercurrents. The same pattern emerges from Donald Davie's comment on 'Sometimes a light surprises' in his Introduction to *The New Oxford Book of Christian Verse*:

> 'Sometimes'—only sometimes, not always, not even very often! The 'holy contemplation' that is thereafter evoked, the sweet security, the unforced adoration—all this is distinctly *not* what any one, it seems, should expect to experience at all often, in church or out of it. It is *not* presented as the normal condition of the Believer. . . . it is only *sometimes*, on one or two Sundays out of many, that 'a light surprises' and the words take on heartfelt meaning, 'while he sings'.[8]

We can see a modern portrait developing here, that of a tentative, hesitant, half-believer; it is part of the way in which, quite naturally, we seek to remake Cowper in our own image. Newey, for instance, would like us to see the hymns in the context of Cowper's other work, and of the 'psycho-drama' of confinement which makes Cowper so close in spirit to our own. And, as an extreme example,

---

[5] Vincent Newey, *Cowper's Poetry* (Liverpool, 1982), p. 287. I am greatly indebted to Mr Newey for reading a draft of this essay, and for making many valuable suggestions.

[6] *Ibid.*, p. 287.

[7] *Ibid.*, p. 296.

[8] Donald Davie, ed., *The New Oxford Book of Christian Verse* (Oxford, 1981), p. xxv.

Erik Routley has said that 'God moves in a mysterious way' was 'written by a man conquered by despair'.[9]

It is not difficult to see how this idea came into being. It began with Samuel Greatheed's discussion of the nervous collapse of 1773 in his memorial sermon for Cowper:

> Our departed friend conceived some presentiment of this sad reverse as it drew near; and during a solitary walk in the fields, he composed a hymn, which is so appropriate to our subject, and so expressive of the faith and hope which he retained so long as he possessed himself. . . .[10]

The presentiment, the solitary walker, the imminent breakdown, all suggest a figure with whom we have become familiar: Cowper as the unfortunate, muddled, bullied Christian, the victim of too much Newton and too much Calvinistic evangelicalism. And yet the *Olney Hymns* do not suggest this (nor do the letters of the same period, from 1767 to 1773). They suggest a figure who has found, however precariously, some kind of assurance; a figure who is quite different from the *angst*-ridden unstable soul of the Cowper myths.

In the face of such complex disagreements and contrary impressions, there seems room for an examination of the hymns themselves. I take as a point of departure the remarks of Bill Hutchings, in his chapter on the *Olney Hymns* in *The Poetry of William Cowper*. Hutchings introduces a further complication by seeing the hymns as stepping stones to the real poetry, successful but only a 'limited form of success'.[11] He also argues that:

> As soon as a writer uses words other than those taken exactly from sanctified material, he is committing himself to solving all the problems of achieving an effective organization of those words. For the development of the hymn, this means that, as soon as he deviates from the exact language of the psalmist, the hymnographer becomes a poet.[12]

I propose to look carefully at Cowper's 'effective organisation' of

[9] Erik Routley, *I'll Praise My Maker* (London, 1951), p. 109.
[10] Quoted in *The Poems of William Cowper*, ed. John D. Baird and Charles Ryskamp (Oxford, 1980), I.484.
[11] Bill Hutchings, *The Poetry of William Cowper* (London, 1982), p. 45.
[12] *Ibid.*, p. 22.

word, image, rhythm, and structure, regarding the *Olney Hymns* not as psycho-drama but as poetry. This is a very different approach from that of Spacks or Newey, who find the strength of the hymns in their psychological insight and rendering of experience; I prefer to suggest that the power of Cowper's hymnody lies not so much in what it says as in the way in which it says it. The psychological insight is commonplace, the heritage of all convertites and believers; but the expression is the unique property of Cowper's own poetic instinct as it engages with the evangelical experience. That evangelical experience cannot be left out, of course, because it is always necessary to remember that Cowper was writing as an eighteenth-century evangelical and not as a proto-existentialist. Some of the qualities of the hymns are owing to the influence of prose writers, poets, and hymnographers, Bunyan, Herbert, Milton, Watts, the classics of a religious and evangelical library. For once the word 'intertextuality' seems appropriate, for their presence is pervasive as well as conscious, second only to the Bible where, as Cowper wrote in 'The Light and Glory of the Word', 'A glory gilds the sacred page,/ Majestic like the sun'. And yet, I shall argue, the result is not just conditioned by the mode of expression, not just an eighteenth-century set of paraphrases and versified experience; it is also a poetry of a high order, in which the words have a life and energy in relation to one another that is profoundly moving and effective.

As a first example we may take Routley's hymn of a despairing man, 'God moves in a mysterious way'. If we look at this without reference to Greatheed's memorial sermon, it is clear that it is not a hymn of despair at all, but one of assurance, of faith in the promises of God. Its title 'Light shining out of darkness' is a reference to John 1:5, but also to numerous other occurrences of light-darkness imagery in the Old Testament (Isaiah 9:2, 60:1) and the New Testament (2 Peter 1:19; 1 Peter 2:19). It is, therefore, a common Biblical image for the working of God in redemption; and yet the hymn begins with the most astonishing line:

God moves in a mysterious way,[13]

which gathers into itself an entirely different set of attributes. How, and in what sense, does God 'move'? If he does move in anything like the usual human sense, he does so 'in a mysterious way', in a manner

[13] All quotations are from the 1779 edition of *Olney Hymns*.

that is un-knowable to human sense. One way of saying this is that he plants his footsteps in the sea (where, of course, they cannot be seen) and rides upon the storm. But 'God moves' also carries the sense that he 'makes moves', he acts, carries out his purposes, has a strategy like a chess player who makes moves. He does so in a way which is unfathomable, mysterious, like a chess player whose moves are so clever and purposeful that his opponent cannot discover them. The first line beautifully articulates these impressions: from 'God moves', apparently so straightforward and simple, monosyllabic, the reader is led to the polysyllabic word 'mysterious', which lengthens out the line with its stress on the second syllable. The effect of 'mysterious' is to complicate wonderfully the first 'God moves', producing a resonance which echoes through the remaining verses of the hymn. Not only are God's movements or actions unknowable; they are also 'mysterious' in another sense. The meaning now is that of a secret practice, some highly technical operation in a trade or art which is therefore designated a mystery. It is this sense which leads Cowper into the bright imagery of the second verse:

> Deep in unfathomable mines
> Of never failing skill;
> He treasures up his bright designs,
> And works his sovereign will.

From the swift-moving God of the first verse, planting his footsteps in the sea and riding on the storm, we turn to a God who is deep within the earth, working like a craftsman or artificer at his 'bright designs' which shine through the darkness of the mine (light shining out of darkness in a more localized form).

Beyond this meaning of 'mystery' is a further meaning, from the later Christian Greek μυστήριον, which was often rendered as 'sacrament', that is the ultimate mystery of God himself, the mystical presence of God, the truth so sacred that, like the Eleusinian mysteries, it is profoundly secret and holy. 'God moves in a mysterious way' thus becomes a movement in a sacred and holy manner, one which is unapproachable, except that its fundamental and mysterious truth is that of mercy, God in redemption:

> Ye fearful saints fresh courage take,
> The clouds ye so much dread
> Are big with mercy, and shall break
> In blessings on your head.

Sea: storm: mines: clouds: the great mystery of God's purposes (his 'movements') is unfolded in the imagery which the poet uses. Each image explores a different aspect of the mysterious and holy God, and it is the imagery which carries the developing meanings through which the word 'mysterious' is differently defined. Cowper's own note to verse 6 line 1 gives a reference to John 13:7:

> Jesus answered and said unto him, What I do thou knowest not now; but thou shalt know hereafter.

This underlines further the kind of mystery that Cowper is concerned to tease out: he is aware of the loving purposes of God, but he knows also that these are often difficult for human beings to understand. Peter's amazed question, 'Lord, dost thou wash my feet?' is an emblematic moment, typical of the partial sight of human beings; they are taken in by appearances, which often belie the reality. So Cowper can use a word such as 'behind' in verse 4:

> Behind a frowning providence,
> He hides a smiling face.

The image is that of a mask, with God as a fatherly figure behind it. The mask has a frown on it, but behind is a benevolent and smiling face, which may be revealed at any time (at the end of the game, so to speak). Similarly the words 'ripen' and 'unfolding' in verse 5 suggest the image which emerges beautifully in the second two lines of the verse (the movement of the verse enacting the emerging):

> The bud may have a bitter taste,
> But sweet will be the flow'r.

In the original version ('But *wait*, to *Smell the flower*'), Cowper has his own fun with the rhythm of the lines, forcing the reader to pause, to play the poet's game: the colloquial, homely force of 'wait' and 'smell' are part of this playfulness, which is lost in the refining of the 1779 printed version. In the manuscript, the sudden stop is part of the sheer delight of this hymn, signalled by the exuberance of its imagery, and by the incongruity (in a pleasing, Metaphysical Poetry sense) of treating the relationship between mankind and Almighty God as, at times, a game with a benevolent father.

The images, the 'big' clouds, the frowning providence, the bitter-tasting bud, are part of this play, because they all hold the promise of the future. Indeed Cowper introduces them in order to give himself room to predict better things, and the future tense is vitally important in this hymn. The clouds 'shall break'; the purposes 'will ripen'; and, above all, God the interpreter 'will make it plain'. The last line of the hymn triumphantly governs the first: the mysteriousness of God's ways will be made clear in the fullness of time. Cowper is echoing Genesis 40:8—'Do not interpretations belong to God?'— but also the New Testament assurance that we shall *know* God: 'now I know in part', writes St Paul, 'but then I shall know even as also I am known' (1 Corinthians 13:12).

The imagery conducts the meaning: it supplies emblems of the power and majesty of God, and the inability of human beings to comprehend his ways. The natural posture before such a God is one of humility, awe, and fear ('ye fearful Saints'), but Cowper acknowledges this only to exhort the faithful to courage. For Cowper (of all people) to be exhorting the fearful Saints to take courage is a feature of the hymn which must not be ignored: the hymn has too frequently been interpreted as an expression of fragility because of the clouds, the frowning providence, and the bitter-tasting bud. But Cowper is introducing these things in order to re-assert the fundamental greatness and benevolence of God; beneath the exhortation there is a quiet confidence, which is felt in the hymn through its rhythms. There are two ways in which this is done, and they complement each other nicely. The first is the steady progression through the four-line verses, so that the sense is amplified throughout and is only complete at the end of the verse:

> Deep in unfathomable Mines,
> Of never failing Skill,
> He treasures up his bright designs,
> And works his Sovereign Will.

This assured and gentle forward movement is delightfully varied by the surprise which Cowper contrives to introduce from time to time. The most obvious example is *'wait,* to *Smell the flower'* which has been already mentioned; but consider the beautiful pauses, the exquisite use of line endings in

> The clouds ye so much dread
> Are big with Mercy, and shall break
> In blessings on your head.

Here the expectations are delicately and delightfully contradicted: the clouds are ... *big*, but big with Mercy, and they will break ... In *blessings*. The hymn abounds in such fine turns of meaning, and it is only because it is so familiar that we do not notice its originality and charm; until finally, the ending eschews surprise in favour of something more simple and decorous:

> God is his own Interpreter
> And he will make it plain.

The straightforward simplicity of the last line is a fitting conclusion to a hymn which has investigated a labyrinth of images and ideas. Now Cowper envisages a time in which all will be revealed, in which concealment, confusion, and ignorance will have been dispelled in the serene light of Heaven (there is even perhaps a reminiscence of 'the crooked shall be made straight, and the rough places plain', from Isaiah 40:4).

It may be attractive to twentieth-century agnostics to see this hymn as one in which Cowper is at breaking-point, but such an interpretation does not fit the poem as we have it. Nevertheless, Cowper is very good at longing, uncertainty, and even desperation; what I wish to argue is that this must be seen within the context of the doctrine of penitence and forgiveness, and that it is not, in itself, evidence of a failure of faith or of trust.

Spacks gives an example of Cowper's apparent weakness when she quotes 'The Contrite Heart':

> The Lord will happiness divine
> On contrite hearts bestow:
> Then tell me, gracious God, is mine
> A contrite heart, or no?

The hymn is a particularly clear example of Cowper's seeming fragility of belief, expressed with humility and candour:

> I sometimes think myself inclin'd
> To love thee, if I could;
> But often feel another mind,
> Averse to all that's good.

> Thy saints are comforted I know,
>   And love thy house of pray'r;
> I therefore go where others go,
>   But find no comfort there.

If we link such verses with Cowper's insanity, the combination suggests a convincing picture of a man under pressure, struggling for repose, desperately searching for faith, and finally driven insane by the evangelical insistence on the conviction of salvation. As a theory this may well fit Cowper himself: nobody knows how much damage the evangelicals did to him, or how much their repellent doctrines upset an already precarious balance. But it does not fit the *Olney Hymns*. Even 'The Contrite Heart' has at its centre the comforting thought that God will save those of a broken heart and be near those of a contrite spirit (Psalm 34:18). Cowper is here producing something very difficult indeed, a hymn of true confession: he has to do so in such terms that he cannot possibly be accused of spiritual pride in his own humility. Very properly, he confesses his own failure to hear the word of God, his lack of love towards God, his weak desires, his feeble worship: above all, perhaps, he does not know whether his heart is broken or not. If he could be sure that he had a contrite heart, he would be able to rejoice, but he cannot:

> Oh make this heart rejoice, or ache;
>   Decide this doubt for me;
> And if it be not broken, break,
>   And heal it, if it be.

The prayer is staggering in its bravery. This final stanza has been described as 'Donnean' by Spacks,[14] and certainly it has a most effective call to God to 'batter' the poet's heart. The bold alliterative patterns, 'decide ... doubt ... broken ... break', help to increase the tension because they lead up to the violent word 'break'. Even the release of tension in the last line is somehow productive of more tension, because it is the tension of uncertainty that is emphasized in the final phrase. But that uncertainty is creative, because there are two ways out: to be broken, and to be healed. Cowper has anticipated the kind of penitential uncertainty which is expressed in T.S. Eliot's *Ash Wednesday*, the uncertainty which is a part of humility and which prevents confession becoming one more kind of self-satisfying religious experience.

---

[14] Spacks, *The Poetry of Vision*, p. 167.

Cowper was powerfully aware of how easily humility can become pride:

> My God! how perfect are thy ways!
>   But mine polluted are;
> Sin twines itself about my praise,
>   And slides into my pray'r.
>
> ('Jehovah our Righteousness')

The serpent image of twining and sliding is neatly controlled, as so many of Cowper's are. Here he faces the baffling problem of pride which enters everywhere, even into praise. Like many others, Marvell and Bunyan among them, Cowper finds this an intractable problem, and sometimes comes to a dead stop:

> How shall I secure my peace,
> And make the Lord my friend?

The lines come from 'The Heart Healed and Changed by Mercy', one of Cowper's most Herbert-like poems. In it sin and fears are embodied and active:

> Sin enslav'd me many years,
>   And led me bound and blind;
> Till at length a thousand fears
>   Came swarming o'er my mind.

He has the help of others, but this proves ineffective; so does the reliance on the law. Cowper is echoing Romans 3 and Galatians 3, and his stabbing simplicities are very close to Herbert in feeling, tone, and rhythm:

> Friends and ministers said much
>   The gospel to enforce;
> But my blindness still was such,
>   I chose a legal course:
> Much I fasted, watch'd and strove,
> Scarce would shew my face abroad,
> Fear'd, almost, to speak or move,
>   A stranger still to God.

The final verse relates how the poet falls at God's feet, and then is broken in spirit—but broken by love, not fear:

> Then my stubborn heart he broke,
> And subdu'd me to his sway;
> By a simple word he spoke,
> 'Thy sins are done away.'

The result is an evangelical equivalent of Herbert's 'The Collar', with the same pattern of struggle followed by a concluding and surprising simplicity. Cowper lacks the sinewy wit of Herbert, the power that comes from compression, but his poem is equally honest in excluding spiritual pride. Cowper has an unerring eye for falsity in religion, not only in his own praise and prayer, but also in the lives of others:

> The Lord receives his highest praise,
> From humble minds and hearts sincere;
> While all the loud professor says,
> Offends the righteous Judge's ear.
> ('A Living and a Dead Faith')

He is severe upon hypocrites (in 'True and False Comforts'), and upon Antinomians:

> Thy Book displays a gracious Light,
> That can the Blind restore,
> But These are dazzled by the Sight,
> And Blinded still the more.
> ('Abuse of the gospel')

He is also severe upon the exultation of newly-converted Christians. Like Bunyan, he knew that conversion was only the beginning, and in 'The New Convert' he writes of 'The new-born child of gospel grace', using the image of the babe-in-arms to denote the infant in a spiritual sense:

> No fears he feels, he sees no foes,
> No conflict yet his faith employs, ...

Cowper's tone is that of a battle-hardened warrior addressing a new recruit:

> When Gideon arm'd his num'rous host,
> The Lord soon made his numbers less;
> And said, lest Israel vainly boast,
> 'My arm procur'd me this success.'

> Thus will he bring our spirits down,
> And draw our ebbing comforts low;
> That sav'd by grace, but not our own,
> We may not claim the praise we owe.

The point about such hymns as 'The New Convert' and 'Abuse of the gospel' is their confidence: Cowper not only has the ability to instruct others in what is true or false, but he also has the strength to expect suffering. He has the courage to see it as part of the necessary process of human and spiritual life: without the slightest trace of cant, he knows that the Christian life is a struggle, and without the slightest trace of pride, he feels its sorrow. It is found, for example, in 'Walking with God', a poem which sees Mrs Unwin's illness of 1767 as demanding Cowper's surrender to the will of God. Only if he agrees to tear the dearest Idol (Mrs Unwin) from his heart will he find a purer light 'That leads me to the Lamb'.

It is this extreme level of intensity which lies behind a dramatic hymn such as 'Hark my soul! it is the Lord'. It is headed by a demanding text, 'Lovest thou me?', from St John's Gospel (21:16), where Jesus speaks these words to Peter. To the evangelicals, the betrayal of Peter, followed by Christ's forgiveness and the command 'Feed my sheep', was a favourite example of God's mercy and trust. Cowper turns the poem into a daring monologue, in which Jesus speaks quietly but insistently to every sinner. The hymn is an intricate interweaving of Old Testament and New Testament images, but its chief poetic skill is in the control which is exercised over these by rhythm and rhyme. Cowper uses the AABB rhyme to set up echoes and contrasts; he divides the lines into half-lines to create a pause followed by a continuation, which gives the impression of gentle pursuit and insistent questioning. The first verse sets the pattern:

> Hark! my soul! it is the Lord;
> 'Tis thy Saviour, hear his word;
> Jesus speaks, and speaks to thee;
> 'Say, poor sinner, lov'st thou me?'

The first line suggests the Fall ('And they heard the voice of the Lord God walking in the garden in the cool of the day', Genesis 3:8), but the second balances this with the redemption: ' 'Tis thy Saviour'. The heavy caesura of the first line creates the expectation of a similar caesura in the second, and this gives an important emphasis to the word 'Saviour'.

Three points of impact occur before the heavy pauses, on 'soul', 'Lord', and 'Saviour', followed by the subsidiary 'word'. This is, of course, Jesus's speech, the word of God, the word as in Holy Scripture itself, but also perhaps a reminder of the word made flesh, Jesus as λόγος. The connection between 'Lord' and 'word' is reinforced by the tight rhyme-scheme, which sets up expectation and counterexpectation: the first line suggests the judgement, the second reminds the reader of mercy. Similarly, the second couplet identifies the central opposition between 'thee' and 'me', human and divine. At other times, Cowper varies the pattern, giving us in verse 2 'bound/wound' and 'right/light', where the first two lines balance the second two, again continuing the pattern of Fall and Redemption. Verse 4 contains another variation:

> Mine is an unchanging love,
> Higher than the heights above;
> Deeper than the depths beneath,
> Free and faithful, strong as death.

Love/above, beneath/death: the combination is spectacular and inclusive. The rhymes suggest an opposition between love, which is above, and death, which is beneath; and yet the strong middle lines make it clear that above and beneath are connected, and through that connection there is also the outer link between love and death. Death, the great changer, is faced by love, the unchanging, and love is as strong as death. Similarly the final verse works across a single, sharp contrast between 'complaint/faint' and 'adore/more'.

The hymn thus works in a variety of one-two patterns: its other chief delight is the delicate patterns of repetition, beginning with the chiasmus

> Hark, my soul, it is the Lord;
> 'Tis thy Saviour, hear his word;

the repetition of 'Hark ... hear' is taken up in the next line, 'Jesus speaks, and speaks to thee'. Now the caesura allows a statement, a pause, and then an amplification, acting out the insistence of the still small voice through its rhythms and placing within the lines. So in the second verse we find:

> I deliver'd thee when bound,
> And, when wounded, heal'd thy wound;
> Sought thee wand'ring, set thee right,
> Turn'd thy darkness into light.'

The two middle lines continue the pattern of repetition, 'wounded . . . wound', 'Sought thee . . . set thee'; outside them are the opposites, deliverance and bondage, darkness and light. Repetition and opposition combine in this hymn: the voice that speaks, and speaks again, tells of tremendous oppositions, of sin and love, of forgetting and remembering, of depth and height, of human love that is weak and faint and divine love that is free and faithful. The alliterative pattern of the last pair is taken up in the next verse:

> Thou shalt see my glory soon,
> When the work of grace is done;

glory . . . grace: the alliteration encompasses the two great attributes of Almighty God who is both judge and Saviour. As Isaac Watts had written:

> How shall affrighted mortals dare
> To show thy glory and thy grace?
> ('God is a name my soul adores', *Horae Lyricae*, 1706)

Glory and grace are a pair here, but a pair which allows Watts to signify in their relationship the whole Christian doctrine of God as majestic creator and God as redeemer. Cowper also works in repetitions and pairings, and the last verses contain both. In the penultimate verse there is the contrast between the two nouns, 'Partner' and 'sinner':

> Partner of my throne shalt be,
> Say, poor sinner, lov'st thou me?

This is followed by the final verse, where the final repetition of 'love thee . . . love thee' takes up the rhetorical pattern for the last time:

> Lord, it is my chief complaint,
> That my love is weak and faint
> Yet I love thee and adore,
> Oh for grace to love thee more!

As so often in Cowper, the control masks an amazing distance: in this case between the first line and the last. The first line sounds as though the writer has a grievance, and indeed one of the surprises of the verse is the turn between the first and second line, when the grievance becomes a self-accusation: thereafter the thrice-repeated 'love' marks a series of steps upward from a weak and faint love, to an adoration, and then to a possibility of grace in which that love can become more.

In addition to this consummate art of pause, rhyme, opposition, and repetition, it should be noted that the hymn is an intricate tissue of Old Testament and New Testament images. This is found throughout Cowper's hymnody. His typographical mind takes an Old Testament text and re-interprets it, giving it life and meaning in the process. In 'Old-Testament Gospel', for instance, he describes how

> Israel in ancient days,
> Not only had a view
> Of Sinai in a blaze,
> But learn'd the gospel too:
> The types and figures were a glass
> In which they saw the Saviour's face.

He uses texts from Leviticus in this hymn, applying them to the emblems of salvation through Jesus Christ; the same process is subtly applied in 'Jehovah-Rophi, I am the Lord that healeth thee'. The text-title comes from Exodus 15:26, but Cowper gives it a New Testament centre:

> Heal us, Emmanuel, here we are,
> Waiting to feel thy touch;

By using 'Emmanuel', God with us, the name given to Jesus by the prophet and fulfilled at his birth as told by St Matthew (1:23), Cowper makes it clear that the Jehovah-healer is now Jesus, whose garment was touched in the crowd by the woman who had an issue of blood (Mark 5:25–34).

The most unusual instance of Cowper's Old Testament and New Testament imagery is 'Praise for the fountain open'd', which has a text from Zechariah 13:1 but which again begins with Emmanuel:

> There is a fountain fill'd with blood
> Drawn from Emmanuel's veins;
> And sinners, plung'd beneath that flood,
> Loose all their guilty stains.

This is an extraordinary example of the way in which Cowper's confident use of words affects his presentation of the gospel. It is deliberately shocking, and it has predictably aroused strong emotions. Hutchings gives two examples, Hugh I'Anson Fausset (who complains of 'the barbarous concomitants of sacrificial suffering inflicted by the God of Evangelicalism') and the parsonical Routley, who calls the first stanza 'crude' but then adds 'the reality is crude':

> Sin is not polite or polished, and the measures which God took for its redemption were not, in earthly terms, fit for fastidious minds to contemplate.[15]

Hutchings, who rightly suggests that neither of these comments is of much help, points out that the first verse has a place in the structure of the hymn as a whole, and that the fourth verse is crucial:

> E'er since, by faith, I saw the stream
> Thy flowing wounds supply:
> Redeeming love has been my theme,
> And shall be till I die.

This marks the beautiful transition from the contemplation of the fountain of blood to the fountains of water, for the hymn is based not only upon Zechariah's vision of the fountain but also upon Isaiah 1:18 ('Though your sins be as scarlet, they shall be as white as snow') and Revelation 7:13–17, where those in white robes 'have washed their robes, and made them white in the blood of the Lamb':

> For the Lamb which is in the midst of the throne shall feed them, and shall lead them unto living fountains of waters: and God shall wipe away all tears from their eyes.

As so often in these hymns, Cowper is handling gigantic contrasts, and the shock of the first line is calculated and necessary. It is the same

---

[15] Routley, *I'll Praise My Maker*, p. 95.

treading on the edge of decorum that is found in Herbert's 'The Agonie':

> all his hair
> His skinne, his garments bloudie be.
> Sinne is that presse and vice, which forceth pain
> To hunt his cruell food through ev'ry vein.

Herbert links this brilliantly with the wine of the Holy Communion; Cowper uses blood as an emblem of salvation:

> Dear dying Lamb, thy precious blood
>   Shall never lose its pow'r;
> Till all the ransom'd church of God
>   Be sav'd, to sin no more.

The first three words are still shocking: the Lamb is the Lamb of Revelation 7, but it is still dying, as if the reader were watching it losing the last of its blood. As we notice this, we become aware of the contrast between present participles and past participles in the hymn: the Lamb is dying, the wounds are flowing, the love is redeeming; opposed to this is the fountain filled, the blood drawn, the sinners plunged, the church ransomed. It can be seen that there is a complex interaction between active and passive, God and man, between the Lamb who dies and redeems and the sinners who are plunged. Plunged by whom?—by the same Lamb who prepares the golden harp, the 'blood-bought free reward':

> 'Tis strung, and tun'd, for endless years,
>   And form'd by pow'r divine;
> To sound, in God the Father's ears,
>   No other name but thine.

The harp, like the player, is made good by God; from a beginning in blood, we move to an end in music. All the human being can do is to wash his sins at the fountain (verse 2) and sing in paradise; the rest (in T.S. Eliot's words) 'is not our business.'[16]

The subtle organization of this hymn is characteristic of Cowper's art. The same control is found in the hymns about Divine Providence, such as 'Wisdom' with its lovely 7.6.7.6.D. rhythm, or 'Joy

---

[16] T.S. Eliot, 'East Coker', section II.

and Peace in Believing', the hymn so rightly admired by Donald
Davie:

> Sometimes a light surprizes
>   The christian while he sings;
> It is the Lord who rises
>   With healing in his wings:
> When comforts are declining,
>   He grants the soul again
> A season of clear shining
>   To cheer it after rain.

The power of this verse is in the feminine rhymes—surprizes/rises,
declining/shining; the second word lifts the first, and this is also
enacted in the sound pattern, when the high 'i' sounds of 'Sometimes
a light surprizes' fall on the heavy syllable of the iambic foot, pushing
the voice upwards as in a musical phrase.

    The images in the first verse are principally to do with light and
sunshine, and they articulate most beautifully the sense of 'inner
weather' that Cowper is describing in the second part of the verse.
The rhyme words declining/again, shining/rain are again particularly important: the 'shining . . . after rain' is notably skilful, for it
gives the end of the verse a visual weather image to act as an emblem
for the idea of God as comforter and provider. The words 'healing',
'season', and 'clear' are all associated with this, and they act as a
counterpoint to the 'n' sounds of the rhymes. Into this Constable-
like landscape of sunshine and rain (Constable was a great admirer of
Cowper) the biblical references and religious themes slip with unob-
trusive skill. In the season of clear shining, the mind turns naturally
to thankfulness:

> In holy contemplation,
>   We sweetly then pursue
> The theme of God's salvation,
>   And find it ever new: . . .

The biblical imagery takes its place in the verse structure with the
maximum of control and the minimum of fuss. Cowper has been
declaring that the Christian can have confidence, whatever the mor-
row may bring (Matthew 6:34):

It can bring with it nothing
  But he will bear us thro';
Who gives the lilies clothing
  Will clothe his people too:
Beneath the spreading heavens,
  No creature but is fed;
And he who feeds the ravens,
  Will give his children bread.

The appeal of this verse is not in its sense (difficult to believe in times of famine) but in the simple neatness of the paraphrase. It is, as Cowper promised, 'sweetly' pursuing its theme: Matthew 6:25–32 is abbreviated, without losing its meaning, and fitted into the verse form without a flicker of strain or hesitation.

Cowper can be controlled and purposeful, or exuberant and extravagant; in either case he seems to know exactly the effect he wishes to produce. As a final example of extravagances (Spacks's word) there is the last of Cowper's hymns in the collection, 'I will praise the Lord at all times'. Spacks is severe on this hymn, saying that the extravagances 'are imperfectly controlled, and likely to alienate rather than to attract the reader';[17] Newey too finds it 'merely a set of logical "religious" equations.'[18] It is worth quoting in full:

Winter has a joy for me,
While the Saviour's charms I read,
Lowly, meek, from blemish free,
In the snow-drop's pensive head.

Spring returns, and brings along
Life-invigorating suns:
Hark! the turtle's plaintive song,
Seems to speak his dying grones!

Summer has a thousand charms,
All expressive of his worth;
'Tis his sun that lights and warms,
His the air that cools the earth.

[17] Spacks, *The Poetry of Vision*, p. 169.
[18] Newey, *Cowper's Poetry*, p. 297.

What! has autumn left to say
Nothing, of a Saviour's grace?
Yes, the beams of milder day
Tell me of his smiling face.

Light appears with early dawn;
While the sun makes haste to rise,
See his bleeding beauties, drawn
On the blushes of the skies.

Ev'ning, with a silent pace,
Slowly moving in the west,
Shews an emblem of his grace,
Points to an eternal rest.

The reason for quoting this hymn in full is that its effect depends principally on its pace, and on its inclusiveness. Its pace is unhurried, its images succeeding one another in a regular procession; its inclusiveness takes into account all times and seasons, indeed all life, and moves inexorably towards the final word 'rest'. The hymn comes to rest at that point: the various times of year, morning and evening, all give way at last to the final end of time and season, in the eternal rest which is given by God's grace.

The appropriate decorum is new, and different. Here it can be seen that Cowper delicately structures the hymn from image to image: he does not wish to do more than point to emblems, season by season—the snowdrop, the turtle's song, the summer sun and the summer breeze, the gentler breath of autumn. Each of these celebrates a quality of the Saviour: his beauty, his sufferings, his power, and his love. Each does so in the same unhurried regularity of the seven-syllable line, which lulls the reader into an acceptance of what seem predictable and traditional attributes. The very simplicity of the concepts is a virtue: the reader's mind does not need to engage in elaborate imaginative manoeuvres to grasp the points as they are made. Then, into this lulling series of similitudes, comes the surprising fifth verse, with its likening of the red dawn to the bleeding beauties of Christ. It is suddenly daring, yet delivered with the same apparent reasonableness as the other comparisons; this forces us to take it more seriously than we might have done, to view it as an amazing attempt to see Christ everywhere, and the world as transfigured by his bleeding beauties, the suffering and redeeming love of the cross. The poem throws up this astonishing verse, and then appropriately returns to its earlier mode. Having seen the vision of the brilliant morning, it now moves slowly to the vision of rest; it is repeating, in its form and imagery, the process of the *nunc dimittis*—'Lord, now lettest thou thy servant depart in peace: according to thy word. For mine eyes have seen thy salvation.'

I have chosen to conclude with this hymn because it has been criticized (even by Spacks and Newey, who are generally sympathetic to Cowper), and because I believe it to be more beautiful and effective than has hitherto been recognized. The same goes for the others: I have tried to show that they are controlled by a subtle and sympathetic poetic intelligence, which relates word to line, image to image, line to verse, rhyme to rhyme, with a considerable conscious and intuitive skill. Truly the hymnographer has become poet.

V

Dickens and the Real World: A Reading of 'The Uncommercial Traveller'

PHILIP DREW

The Uncommercial Traveller was the title Dickens gave to a series of papers which he published at intervals in *All the Year Round* between 1859 and 1867. They are thus, though late in his career, of a somewhat similar type to the early essays collected under the title *Sketches by Boz*, with the obvious and important difference that Dickens was now the editor of the periodical for which he was writing. He originally collected seventeen essays and published them in 1860, adding a further eleven for the cheap edition of 1865. The Illustrated Library edition, which first appeared in 1875, added eight more essays and the Gad's Hill edition (1890) one more, making thirty-seven in all. It is this collection to which all references are made.

The Uncommercial Traveller was reasonably well received in its early forms,[1] but since then its neglect has been almost complete. *Dickens and the Twentieth Century*, edited by John Gross and Gabriel Pearson (London, 1962), does not even mention it in the index, most references in general works are perfunctory or dismissive, while one of the very few recent treatments, that in Gordon Spence's *Charles Dickens as a Familiar Essayist* (Salzburg, 1977), gives little more than a description of the contents. It is safe to say that today hardly a reader of Dickens could name the title of a single essay, except possibly 'Dullborough Town' (XII), which deals with the scenes of the author's youth and has therefore interested his biographers.

I shall argue that this neglect is unjustified, since we can find in these essays a side of Dickens's genius which is not given full expression in the novels. In many of them, of course, he remains within fairly familiar territory. He deals more than once with the awfulness of the cooking in British hotels, as for example in 'Refreshments for Travellers' (VI) and 'A Little Dinner in an Hour' (XXXIII), and writes frequently about the actual processes of travelling as in

---

[1] The favourable review in the *Saturday Review* XI (23 February 1861) is reprinted in *Dickens: The Critical Heritage* ed. Philip Collins (London, 1971), where it is attributed to James Fitzjames Stephen.

'Aboard Ship' (XXXI) and 'The Calais Night Mail' (XVIII). But
Dickens has indicated from the beginning that his interest in travel is
to be given a wider application. In the first essay, 'His General Line of
Business' (I), he distinguishes himself from the commercial traveller:

> I am rarely to be found in a gig, and am never to be encountered by
> a pleasure train, waiting on the platform of a branch station, quite
> a Druid in the midst of a light Stonehenge of samples. And yet . . . I
> am both a town traveller and a country traveller, and am always
> on the road. Figuratively speaking, I travel for the great house of
> Human Interest Brothers, and have rather a large connection in
> the fancy goods way. Literally speaking, I am always wandering
> here and there from my rooms in Covent-garden, London—now
> about the city streets: now, about the country by-roads—seeing
> many little things, and some great things, which, because they
> interest me, I think may interest others. These are my brief
> credentials as the Uncommercial Traveller.

The idea of travel as a means of, or as a metaphor for, discovery
and exploration lies behind many of the essays: they are in the strict
sense occasional journalism, being Dickens's account of his own
investigation of a matter of topical interest, or his description and
assessment of a new attempt to solve a social problem, and have one
of the most valuable qualities of journalism, but one which we
should perhaps be surprised to find in Dickens, and that is objectiv-
ity. This may be illustrated from one of the earliest essays, 'Wapping
Workhouse' (III). He describes in an amusing but unemphatic
fashion a walk, apparently casual and directionless, through the East
End of London. It then emerges that the journey is not altogether an
idle ramble. 'No, I was going to Wapping, because an Eastern police
magistrate had said, through the morning papers, that there was no
classification at the Wapping workhouse for women, and that it was
a disgrace and a shame, and divers other hard names, and because I
wished to see how the fact really stood.' He indicates that his visit is
not a specially prepared one—'The Traveller (the matron intimated)
should see the worst first. He was welcome to see everything. Such
as it was, there it all was.'—and describes 'the Foul wards' as he
found them

> in a building most monstrously behind the time—a mere series of
> garrets or lofts, with every inconvenient and objectionable cir-
> cumstance in their construction, and only accessible by steep and

narrow staircases, infamously ill-adapted for the passage up-stairs
of the sick or down-stairs of the dead.

A-bed in these miserable rooms, here on bedsteads, there (for a
change, as I understood it) on the floor, were women in every
stage of distress and disease. None but those who have attentively
observed such scenes, can conceive the extraordinary variety of
expression still latent under the general monotony and uniformity
of colour, attitude, and condition. The form a little coiled up and
turned away, as though it had turned its back on this world for
ever; the uninterested face at once lead-coloured and yellow,
looking passively upward from the pillow; the haggard mouth a
little dropped, the hand outside the coverlet, so dull and indifferent, so light, and yet so heavy; these were on every pallet;
but when I stopped beside a bed, and said ever so slight a word to
the figure lying there, the ghost of the old character came into the
face, and made the Foul ward as various as the fair world. No one
appeared to care to live, but no one complained; all who could
speak, said that as much was done for them as could be done there,
that the attendance was kind and patient, that their suffering was
very heavy, but they had nothing to ask for. The wretched rooms
were as clean and sweet as it is possible for such rooms to be; they
would become a pest-house in a single week, if they were ill-kept.

He visits next 'a better kind of loft devoted to the idiotic and the
imbecile'. It is plain that he finds the whole place unpleasant, yet the
use of the words 'idiotic and imbecile' indicates that he accepts the
kinds of classifications that underlie the establishment and considers
his primary task to report on whether the establishment itself is run
as decently as can be expected. At times he offers a more complicated
picture:

Everybody else in the room had fits, except the wards-woman; an
elderly, able-bodied pauperess, with a large upper lip, and an air of
repressing and saving her strength, as she stood with her hands
folded before her, and her eyes slowly rolling, biding her time for
catching or holding somebody. This civil personage ... said,
'They has 'em continiwal, sir. They drops without no more notice
than if they was coach-horses dropped from the moon, sir. And
when one drops, another drops, and sometimes there'll be as
many as four or five on 'em at once, dear me, a rolling and a
tearin', bless you—this young woman, now, has 'em dreadful
bad.'

She turned up this young woman's face with her hand as she
said it. This young woman was seated on the floor, pondering in

the foreground of the afflicted. There was nothing repellent either in her face or head.... When I had spoken to her a little, she still sat with her face turned up, pondering, and a gleam of the mid-day sun shone in upon her.

—Whether this young woman, and the rest of these so sorely troubled, as they sit or lie pondering in their confused dull way, ever get mental glimpses among the motes in the sunlight, of healthy people and healthy things? Whether this young woman, brooding like this in the summer season, ever thinks that some-where there are trees and flowers, even mountains and the great sea? Whether, not to go so far, this young woman ever has any dim revelation of that young woman—that young woman who is not here and never will come here; who is courted, and caressed, and loved, and has a husband, and bears children, and lives in a home, and who never knows what it is to have this lashing and tearing coming upon her? And whether this young woman, God help her, gives herself up then and drops like a coach-horse from the moon?

I hardly knew whether the voices of infant children, penetrating into so hopeless a place, made a sound that was pleasant or painful to me. It was something to be reminded that the weary world was not all aweary, and was ever renewing itself; but, this young woman was a child not long ago, and a child not long hence might be such as she.

He visits the nurseries and the 'Refractories', whom he finds picking oakum. 'They sat in line on a form, with their backs to a window; before them, a table, and their work.' This spare sentence is the introduction to a lively dialogue between two of the refractory women and the matron, in which Dickens presents the girls as muddled and hostile. He visits the old and infirm women, and comments sadly, 'From some of the windows, the river could be seen with all its life and movement; the day was bright, but I came upon no one who was looking out.'

The visit concludes with the following paragraph:

The object of my journey was accomplished when the nimble matron had no more to show me. As I shook hands with her at the gate, I told her that I thought Justice had not used her very well, and that the wise men of the East were not infallible.

At one level Dickens appears to have made his inspection and delivered his final report, but his concluding pages are by no means uncritical. He compares the provision at Wapping unfavourably with that in Boston, and observes tartly that without equalization of the Poor-rate between the richer and the poorer London parishes the deficiencies which he has observed can never be eradicated. His final sentences, appended almost without comment, take the form of a dialogue between himself and a pauper in another workhouse altogether:

> 'I beg your pardon, sir,' he had said, in a confidential manner, on another occasion, taking me aside; 'but I have seen better days.'
> 'I am very sorry to hear it.'
> 'Sir, I have a complaint to make against the master.'
> 'I have no power here, I assure you. And if I had—'
> 'But, allow me, sir, to mention it, as between yourself and a man who has seen better days, sir. The master and myself are both masons, sir, and I make him the sign continually; but, because I am in this unfortunate position, sir, he won't give me the counter-sign!'

The presentation of himself as an impartial witness, equally ready to be impressed or dismayed, is reflected in the balanced prose, alive to the comic possibilities of workhouse life yet subduing them to his sense of individual suffering and the practical difficulties of relieving it.

In 'Two Views of a Cheap Theatre' (IV), Dickens takes us once more to the East End, where a new theatre, the Britannia at Hoxton, has been expressly designed for a mass audience. His praise is lavish—'Magnificently lighted by a firmament of sparkling chandeliers, the building was ventilated to perfection ... Its form is beautiful, and the appearance of the audience ... is highly remarkable in its union of vastness with compactness.' He compares it to the Scala at Milan, the San Carlo, and the Paris Opera, and then describes a Saturday evening there. The audience is mixed:

> Among our dresses there were most kinds of shabby and greasy wear, and much fustian and corduroy that was neither sound nor fragrant ... Besides prowlers and idlers, we were mechanics, dock-labourers, costermongers, petty tradesmen, small clerks, milliners, stay-makers, shoe-binders, slop-workers, poor workers in a hundred highways and byways. Many of us—on the whole, the majority—were not at all clean, and not at all choice in our lives or conversation. But we had all come together in a place where our

convenience was well consulted, and where we were well looked after, to enjoy an evening's entertainment in common. We were not going to lose any part of what we had paid for through anybody's caprice, and as a community we had a character to lose. So, we were closely attentive, and kept excellent order; and let the man or boy who did otherwise instantly get out from this place, or we would put him out with the greatest expedition.

The evening consisted of an interminable pantomime with certain concessions to realism and a Melodrama of high moral tone. In the interval the audience recruited themselves on sandwiches 'as substantial as was consistent with portability'. 'Virtue never looked so beautiful or Vice so deformed as when we paused, sandwich in hand, to consider what would come of that resolution of Wickedness in boots, to sever Innocence in flowered chintz from Honest Industry in striped stockings.' Lying behind the familiar humours at the expense of dramatic convention is the serious question of how to entertain, wholesomely, a massive working-class audience. 'I must add that [the proprietor's] sense of the responsibility on him to make the best of his audience, and to do his best for them, is a highly agreeable sign of the times.' Dickens can say this without condescension or hypocrisy because he is prepared to give an unprejudiced account of the proceedings, with all their virtues and all their imperfections.

But a more remarkable balance is yet to be struck, for the distinctive feature of the Britannia was that on Sundays it was used for religious meetings. Accordingly Dickens returns to the theatre the following night and notes with admiration a congregation of four thousand people. So far all is well, but he at once detects and attacks, what he has always rejected, 'the slang and twang of the conventicle, as bad in its way as that of the House of Commons, and nothing worse can be said of it'. In his deadliest vein Dickens illustrates and derides the patronizing falseness of the preacher, who betrays his lack of understanding of the general mind and character of his audience. On the other hand Dickens makes a point of acknowledging the soundness of his message, 'the large Christianity of his general tone'. Justice must be done, even to a man in many respects misguided and ridiculous. Similarly justice compels Dickens to report accurately on the composition of the audience:

I am brought to the fact, that the lowest part of the audience of the previous night, *was not there*. There is no doubt about it. There was no such thing in that building, that Sunday evening. I have been told since, that the lowest part of the audience of the Victoria Theatre has been attracted to its Sunday services. I have been very glad to hear it, but on this occasion of which I write, the lowest part of the usual audience of the Britannia Theatre, decidedly and unquestionably stayed away. When I first took my seat and looked at the house, my surprise at the change in its occupants was as great as my disappointment.

Again and again Dickens makes plain his readiness to revise his initial judgements, 'to the rout and overthrow of all my expectations'. The Victualler in 'Poor Mercantile Jack' (V) is at first presented as an object of suspicion, but in the end Dickens concludes that sailors might do worse than entrust themselves to his care. In the same essay Dickens introduces the negro sailors as if they represented some sinister trap, but eventually acknowledges their singular innocence. He concludes his account of the Mormon emigrants by saying,

What is in store for the poor people on the shores of the Great Salt Lake, what happy delusions they are labouring under now, on what miserable blindness their eyes may be opened then, I do not pretend to say. But I went on board their ship to bear testimony against them if they deserved it, as I fully believed they would; to my great astonishment they did not deserve it; and my predispositions and tendencies must not affect me as an honest witness.
(XXII)

In 'The Great Tasmania's Cargo' (VIII) he writes, 'I believe there never was a more truthful witness than the sergeant. He had no inclination to make out a case.' The same is true of the author. He is quite unable to accept the official exoneration of those responsible for the sufferings of the returning soldiers and the deaths of sixty more. Yet even here, when his principal conclusion is that those in authority have behaved heartlessly and with infamous dishonesty, he is concerned to place blame only where it is due.

Earlier in the same essay, describing one of the more distressing sights, he had commented, 'I had an instinctive feeling that it was not well to turn away, merely to spare myself.' What is impressive about *The Uncommercial Traveller* is Dickens's resolute insistence on seeing what is to be seen and describing it 'with scrupulous exactness': it gives the book its quality of solid circumstance, the living facts recorded by an accurate eye. 'On an Amateur Beat' (XXXV) illustrates very clearly this openness to the play of events. Dickens, setting out for a daytime walk from Covent-garden to Limehouse and Stepney, describes his own methods—'On such an occasion it is my habit to regard my walk as my beat, and myself as a higher sort of police-constable doing duty on the same.' The fruits of his constabulary vigilance are mixed, but this is because he is prepared to report what he finds, not what he hopes or expects to find. First he dismisses contemptuously the current police practice of testifying that certain areas of London are too dangerous for anyone to enter. In his novels, as I have remarked elsewhere,[2] the police force is normally the only profession for which Dickens allows himself to express respect and admiration. In *The Uncommercial Traveller*, while still approving in general of the man in uniform 'employed at twenty shillings a week', he is much readier to criticize the conduct of individual policemen, and in particular the political directives under which they feel obliged to work. Next in the course of his walk he stumbles against a ragged barefooted child. As he tries to comfort 'it' and put money into its 'claw' he is surrounded by a horde of fifty naked hungry children forming 'an obscene scuffle in the mud, of rags and legs and arms and dirt'. A police constable appears, the children scatter, and the constable wipes his forehead, having done all that duty requires of him. Dickens looks at the traces in the mud and wonders whether some future archaeologist finding them petrified could possibly deduce from them 'such an astounding inference as the existence of a polished state of society that bore with the public savagery of neglected children in the streets of its capital city, and was proud of its power by sea and land, and never used its power to seize and save them!'

He proceeds Eastwards, noting the invisible but critical demarcation lines between one neighbourhood and another, including the differences between penny buns east and west of Houndsditch Church. He records an encounter between a mongrel and a woman with a shockingly deformed spine, which he describes as unsentimentally as he had already described goitres in 'Travelling Abroad' (VII), or dead children in 'Dullborough Town' (XII) and 'Some Recollections of Mortality' (XIX). One of the objects of his journey is to look again at the Children's Hospital about which he had written in 'A Small Star in the East' (XXXII), an essay which had handled two linked themes, poverty and industrial disease in Stepney

[2] In *The Meaning of Freedom* (Aberdeen Univ. Press, 1982).

and the establishment of a children's hospital in East London.[3] It is one of the major essays in the collection, and Dickens here recalls it to the mind of his readers as a particularly good demonstration of what can be done by private initiative to relieve the suffering of very poor children. In the remainder of 'On an Amateur Beat' he again takes up a theme from the earlier essay, that of the health of the women who work in the local lead-mills. He describes the processes of converting pig-lead into white-lead in considerable technical detail, taking care to mention the heat and the smell and the danger from contact with particles of lead. At the same time he gives an account of the precautions which are taken, and comments, 'I made it out to be indubitable that the owners of these lead-mills honestly and sedulously try to reduce the dangers of the occupation to the lowest point.' He observes, 'A washing-place is provided for the women,' and adds a characteristic parenthesis, 'I thought there might have been more towels.' He concludes

> American inventiveness would seem to indicate that before very long white-lead may be made entirely by machinery. The sooner, the better. In the meantime, I parted from my two frank conductors over the mills, by telling them that they had nothing there to be concealed, and nothing to be blamed for.

The sentence which most clearly conveys Dickens's receptive attitude in the major social essays occurs in 'Shy Neighbourhoods' (X)—'I wonder at nothing concerning them, and take them as they are.' This is neither a typically Dickensian sentence, nor a sentence with a typically Dickensian run to it. But if it does not suggest Dickens in its stance and disposition, then whom? Hazlitt, perhaps? Of Dickens's aim as a reporter it is fair to ask whether he is trying to give the impression of accuracy which comes from an immediate unrefined registering of experience or that which comes from a careful sifting and selecting and balancing of the facts. Either can impart its own kind of bias. Best of all is a deliberately uncategorized report from someone with no axe to grind who is deeply experienced in assessing situations—'I wished to see how the fact really stood'— so that within the limits of the form it is unselective in presentation of

[3] It was of this essay that Dickens wrote to Mrs James Fields, 'I have described, *with exactness*, the poor places into which I went, and how the people behaved, and what they said.' (Letter of 16 December 1868)

fact—'Such as it was, there it all was'—yet critical of what is reported—'I thought there might have been more towels.'

Dickens then is writing neither as a feuilletonist, inventing material that can be worked up into a number, nor as a journalist looking for an incident that will cause a scandal or a sensation, but as a serious social commentator. He had, of course, from *Pickwick* onwards, realized that his readers could always be persuaded to share his own feelings of indignation about the inadequacies of Victorian society, especially in the treatment of the multiplying urban poor. The difference is that in *The Uncommercial Traveller* he does not generalize about what is wrong. Instead he embarks on the far more difficult enterprise of drawing attention to a small thing being done right, either *ad hoc* (e.g. II), or as an innovation or on a small scale (e.g. XXI and XXV). By their nature these local initiatives will seem humdrum and the praise of them equally insipid, but they are put before the reader as the beginnings of a way forward by intelligence and dedication, a small star in the East.

Although the distresses of the mass of the poor are almost overwhelming, on every side people of good will may be discovered ingeniously and selflessly working to relieve them and are therefore as individuals entitled to the highest commendation. This conviction helps to explain why we encounter so frequently in *The Uncommercial Traveller* a sketch of a person in a position of responsibility performing his work humanely and conscientiously. In the second of the essays we have the 'kind wholesome face' of the 'good Christian minister' who comforts the relatives of the five hundred people drowned in *The Royal Charter*. In 'The Great Tasmania's Cargo' (VIII) the sergeant 'of very intelligent countenance' is precisely the sort of impartial witness that Dickens himself sets out to be in the essays. The 'good hand and the good heart' of the Chairman of the Stepney Board of Guardians in 'The Short-timers' (XXI) is praised as readily as the 'disinterested and wise' arrangements for providing working men with cheap food in 'The Boiled Beef of New England' (XXV) or the 'simplicity and humanity' of the accommodation in a newly built troopship in 'Chatham Dockyard' (XXVI). Readers of the novels will not need to be reminded how uncommon such commendations are in Dickens's fiction.

If this were all, the essays might be regarded as untypical but not particularly interesting tributes to the virtues of Victorian Britain, ministering to the complacency of the subscribers to *All the Year Round*. But, as I have said, Dickens has taken considerable care to ensure that his work cannot be read in this way. In particular, the balance which he is so much concerned to maintain is not simply a matter of prose style but a deliberate weighing of what is good and what is bad. In essay XXV, 'The Boiled Beef of New England', for example, he has nothing but praise for the enterprise that provides cheap meals in Whitechapel, but deplores the monotony of the bill of fare and is ruthless as soon as he thinks he detects in the prohibition of beer a hint of a patronizing attitude to the working man, as if he were 'called by Providence to walk all his days in a station in life represented on festive occasions by a mug of warm milk-and-water and a bun'. Similarly he allows himself an Arnoldian aside quietly regretting the fact that the establishment calls itself The Self-Supporting Cooking Depôt.

Dickens never ignores the massive scale of the suffering, but he never forgets that the victims are men and women:

> ... a drizzling November day. A squalid maze of streets, courts, and alleys of miserable houses let out in single rooms. A wilderness of dirt, rags, and hunger. A mud-desert, chiefly inhabited by a tribe from whom employment has departed, or to whom it comes but fitfully and rarely. They are not skilled mechanics in any wise. They are but labourers,—dock-labourers, water-side labourers, coal-porters, ballast-heavers, such-like hewers of wood and drawers of water. But they have come into existence, and they propagate their wretched race.

The obvious temptation is to simplify the problems by treating the working classes as children, especially in matters of drink. Yet Dickens sees clearly that unless men are recognized as adults, each with his individual hopes and needs, none of the proposed solutions will work. His faith in party politicians, never great, has now turned to bitter contempt. The final irony of the depressing scene described above is the presence of election posters, urging the 'free and independent starvers to vote for Thisman and vote for Thatman.' He continues:

> Pondering in my mind the far-seeing schemes of Thisman and Thatman, and of the public blessing called Party, for staying the degeneracy, physical and moral, of many thousands (who shall say how many?) of the English race; for devising employment useful to the community for those who want but to work and live;

for equalising rates, cultivating waste lands, facilitating emigra-
tion, and, above all things, saving and utilising the oncoming
generations, and thereby changing ever-growing national weakness into strength: pondering in my mind, I say, these hopeful
exertions, I turned down a narrow street to look into a house or
two.

As he implies in 'Medicine Men of Civilisation' (XXVIII), profes-
sional politicians are engaged in a solemn masquerade: nowhere in
the essays is it suggested that they have the will or the ability to
remedy the ills about them. Even the primary purpose of Govern-
ment, which is to take the necessity of maintaining law and order out
of the hands of individual citizens, is weakly and incompetently
carried out. It will not surprise readers of *Little Dorrit* to discover that
Dickens is at his harshest and most uncompromising when he deals
with crime, as in 'The Ruffian' (XXX), and with vagrancy, as in
'Tramps' (XI). The effect of 'The Ruffian' is, as Dickens was well
aware, derived from its deliberate intemperance of tone. While his
criticism of the laxity of the police is softened by his recognition that
they receive no official encouragement to vigilance, his condemna-
tion of cowardly magistrates is unqualified and his detestation of the
habitual criminal is expressed without any attempt at moderation. It
is interesting to note that in this essay he goes out of his way to
declare his support for Carlyle's account of behaviour in the streets of
London. What infuriates Dickens and drives him beyond all
restraints of language and human sympathy is his consciousness that
the lawless activities he describes are carried on not in some bandit-
infested wilderness, but in 'that solitary mountain-spur of the
Abruzzi, the Waterloo Road'. His travels take him to Italy and France
and the Low Countries, to Liverpool and Wales and Brighton and
Chatham, but the weight of them derives from his study of life in
London. The streets of the city where the modern world displayed all
its triumphs and its splendours were also, for Dickens, 'the streets of
a city where every stone seemed to call to me, as I walked along,
"Turn this way, man, and see what waits to be done!"' (III)
I must acknowledge that I have so far been partial in my treatment
of *The Uncommercial Traveller*. My concern has been to draw attention to the seriousness of Dickens's purposes in the major essays, and
to that end I have deliberately emphasized those which bear least
resemblance to Dickens as we encounter him in the novels or in the
mild domesticities of *Reprinted Pieces*. But the collection is large and

various. There are essays rich in sentiment, such as 'The Italian Prisoner' (XI), and a number of reflective essays, perhaps written as a deliberate reminiscence of Lamb, such as 'City of London Churches' (IX), 'Arcadian London' (XVI), and 'The City of the Absent' (XXIII). Similarly Dickens's comic gifts have ample room for expression: 'Shy Neighbourhoods' (X) for example is superficially not unlike one of the *Sketches by Boz*, but gives a much stronger impression of the realities of London life, and finishes with a wonderfully heightened description of a couple of fowls in Bethnal-green, a tour de force of Dickens's mature comic style. It is tempting to dwell on the Trollopian world of 'Titbull's Almshouses' (XXIX), or on the entertaining pictures of legal London in 'Chambers' (XIV), or on the two ferocious fairy tales recounted with unflagging energy and delight in 'Nurse's Stories' (XV). The picture of the grovelling Bully Globson in 'Birthday Celebrations' (XX) is like a sparkling paragraph from one of the early novels, while the portrait of the proprietor of an unsuccessful inn is in Dickens's finest manner:

Before the waitress had shut the door, I had forgotten how many stage-coaches she said used to change horses in the town every day. But it was of little moment; any high number would do as well as another. It had been a great stage-coaching town in the great stage-coaching times, and the ruthless railways had killed and buried it . . .

'*I* don't care for the town,' said J. Mellows . . .; 'I wish I had never seen the town!'

'You don't belong to it, Mr. Mellows?'

'Belong to it!' repeated Mellows. 'If I didn't belong to a better style of town than this, I'd take and drown myself in a pail.' It then occurred to me that Mellows, having so little to do, was habitually thrown back on his internal resources—by which I mean the Dolphin's cellar.

'What we want,' said Mellows . . .; 'what we want, is a Branch. The Petition for the Branch Bill is in the coffee-room. Would you put your name to it? Every little helps.'. Having achieved this . . . I asked Mr. Mellows if he could grace my dinner with a pint of good wine? Mr. Mellows thus replied:

'If I couldn't give you a pint of good wine, I'd—there!—I'd take and drown myself in a pail. But I was deceived when I bought this business, and the stock was higgledy-piggledy, and I haven't yet tasted my way quite through it with a view to sorting it. Therefore, if you order one kind and get another, change till it comes right. For what,' said Mellows . . . 'what would you or any

gentleman do, if you ordered one kind of wine and was required
to drink another? Why, you'd (and naturally and properly, having
the feelings of a gentleman), you'd take and drown yourself in a
pail!'   ('An Old Stage-coaching House' XXIV)

What all the essays have in common is that they are, a few pages
excepted, written in a style quite free from the worst mannerisms of
Dickens's fictional prose. The rhetorical over-emphasis, the polysyllabic facetiousness, the relentless animism of the novels are scarcely
to be found. In their place is a prose of unusual firmness, economy,
and weight. It is difficult to illustrate, since many of the essays owe
their strength not to any passages of singular power but to a control
and consistency of style, but one or two representative passages may
convey these qualities. In the following extract he describes, not for
the first time, a visit to the Paris morgue:

It was strange to see so much heat and uproar seething about one
poor spare white-haired old man, quiet for evermore. He was
calm of feature and undisfigured, as he lay on his back—having
been struck upon the hinder part of the head, and thrown
forward—and something like a tear or two had started from the
closed eyes, and lay wet upon the face. The uncommercial
interest, sated at a glance, directed itself upon the striving crowd
on either side and behind: wondering whether one might have
guessed, from the expression of those faces merely, what kind of
sight they were looking at. The differences of expression were not
many. There was a little pity, but not much, and that mostly with
a selfish touch in it—as who would say, 'Shall I, poor I, look like
that, when the time comes!' There was more of a secretly brooding contemplation and curiosity, as 'That man I don't like, and
have the grudge against; would such be his appearance, if
someone—not to mention names—by any chance gave him an
ugly knock?' There was a wolfish stare at the object . . . and there
was a much more general, purposeless, vacant staring at it—like
looking at waxwork, without a catalogue, and not knowing what
to make of it. But all these expressions concurred in possessing the
one underlying expression of *looking at something that could not
return a look*.   ('Some Recollections of Mortality' XIX)

. . . There was a remarkably agreeable smell of pomatum in this
congregation. But, in other cases, rot and mildew and dead citi-

zens formed the uppermost scent, while, infused into it in a dreamy way not at all displeasing, was the staple character of the neighbourhood. In the churches about Mark-lane, for example, there was a dry whiff of wheat; and I accidentally struck an airy sample of barley out of an aged hassock in one of them. From Rood-lane to Tower-street, and thereabouts, there was often a subtle flavour of wine: sometimes, of tea. One church near Mincing-lane smelt like a druggist's drawer. Behind the Monument the service had a flavour of damaged oranges, which, a little further down towards the river, tempered into herrings, and gradually toned into a cosmopolitan blast of fish. In one church... there was no speciality of atmosphere, until the organ shook a perfume of hides all over us from some adjacent warehouse.

... In all those dusty registers that the worms are eating, there is not a line but made some hearts leap, or some tears flow, in their day. Still and dry now, still and dry! and the old tree at the window with no room for its branches, has seen them all out. So with the tomb of the old Master of the old Company, on which it drips. His son restored it and died, his daughter restored it and died, and then he had been remembered long enough, and the tree took possession of him, and his name cracked out.

There are few more striking indications of the changes of manners and customs that two or three hundred years have brought about, than these deserted churches ... No one can be sure of the coming time; but it is not too much to say of it that it has no sign in its outsetting tides, of the reflux to these churches of their congregations and uses.   ('City of London Churches' IX)

Once—it was after leaving the Abbey and turning my face north—I came to the great steps of St. Martin's church as the clock was striking Three. Suddenly, a thing that in a moment more I should have trodden on without seeing, rose up at my feet with a cry of loneliness and houselessness, struck out of it by the bell, the like of which I never heard. We then stood face to face looking at one another, frightened by one another. The creature was like a beetle-browed hair-lipped youth of twenty, and it had a loose bundle of rags on, which it held together with one of its hands. It shivered from head to foot, and its teeth chattered, and as it stared at me—persecutor, devil, ghost, whatever it thought me—it made with its whining mouth as if it were snapping at me, like a worried dog. Intending to give this ugly object money, I put out my hand to stay it—for it recoiled as it whined and snapped—and laid my hand upon its shoulder. Instantly, it twisted out of its garment, like the young man in the New

Testament, and left me standing alone with its rags in my hands.
('Night Walks' XIII)

At present the essays are noticed chiefly because they furnish some
autobiographical hints: the beginning of 'Travelling Abroad' (VII)
and 'A Fly-leaf in a Life' (XXXVI) derive directly from Dickens's
own youthful and later experiences. 'Dullborough Town' (XII) is a
more complex reflection on the Rochester of his childhood, revisited
in the years of his fame:

> The coach that had carried me away, was melodiously called
> Timpson's Blue-Eyed Maid, and belonged to Timpson, at the
> coach-office up-street; the locomotive engine that had brought
> me back, was called severely No. 97, and belonged to S.E.R., and
> was spitting ashes and hot water over the blighted ground.
> ... When I went alone to the Railway to catch my train at night
> ... I was in a more charitable mood with Dullborough than I had
> been all day; and yet in my heart I had loved it all day too. Ah! who
> was I that I should quarrel with the town for being changed to me,
> when I myself had come back, so changed, to it! All my early
> readings and early imaginations dated from this place, and I took
> them away so full of innocent construction and guileless belief,
> and I brought them back so worn and torn, so much the wiser and
> so much the worse!

Although I have tried to draw attention in this paper to the virtues
of Dickens as a writer of non-fictional prose, he remains inevitably
with most readers as a novelist: the obvious question to ask is
whether a consideration of *The Uncommercial Traveller* is likely to
modify, for better or for worse, our reading of the novels. I think that
it is unlikely to induce any major change. As I have indicated,
Dickens is adopting in the essays a deliberate stance and style: we
may be reminded here of *Little Dorrit* and there of *Our Mutual Friend*
or *Edwin Drood*, but in general Dickens is consciously working in a
different and in many ways more difficult medium. We may therefore indeed come away from the essays with an enhanced opinion of
Dickens's technical powers and intellectual grasp. The comparisons
that are prompted by *The Uncommercial Traveller* are more naturally
with social critics, with Arnold, or Shaw, or Samuel Butler, or, in the
resolute refusal to see only one side of a case, with Carlyle or Ruskin.
In the rapid sizing up of a mechanically complex operation only
Kipling comes to mind as a rival. But such parallels serve to indicate

the scope of the essays, rather than their force. For that we must return to *The Uncommercial Traveller* itself, a work which deserves to be recognized as that of a master of English prose at the height of his powers exhibiting the life of his own city, his own country, and his own society with the selflessness that eschews all stylistic display.

VI

Continuity and Innovation in Victorian English

K.C. PHILLIPPS

In all considerations of semantics, we must bear in mind the important proviso of Susie Tucker in her study of the word *enthusiasm*:[1] 'as long as we remember that nobody wakes up on one New Year's Day partly forgetting sense A and prepared to use a word only in sense AB, and then at a later date forgetting this modification of the older sense and using only sense B'. From the time of the Regency to that of Queen Victoria, there is, as always, gradualness of change, and much overlap of meaning.

Sometimes, however, we can detect the tiredness of an old meaning contrasted with the vigour of a new. Thus, in *A Shabby Genteel Story* Thackeray re-works the idea of Sheridan's Mrs Candour in *The School for Scandal*, who spreads scandal under the guise of being 'candid'; that is, in the older sense of the word, 'charitable'. Thackeray makes a certain Lord *Candour* say

> Yes, yes, ... a sad pity indeed;—dreadfully extravagant, I'm told—bad health—expensive family—works going down every day. (ch. 3)

This is still nominally *OED candour* sense 4, 'freedom from malice, favourable disposition, kindliness', to which the Dictionary adds Johnson's definition 'sweetness of temper, kindness'. But already in Thackeray's day the modern meaning was available: 'freedom from reserve in one's statements ... outspokenness' (*OED* sense 5); and this is vigorously asserted when, in *Middlemarch*, George Eliot recalls the language of her Midlands girlhood:

> To be *candid*, in Middlemarch phraseology, meant to use an early opportunity of letting your friends know that you did not take a

[1] Susie I. Tucker, *Enthusiasm: A Study in Semantic Change* (Cambridge, 1972), p. 162.

cheerful view of their capacity, their conduct, or their position;
and a robust *candour* never waited to be asked for its opinion.
(ch. 74)

The makers of the Dictionary, like all lexicographers, were loth to
categorize any meaning as obsolete;[2] but they do tell us that *expensive*
used, as probably in the Thackeray quotation above, of people in the
sense of 'extravagant' is 'now rare'. The sense occurred quite freely in
the first half of the century; for example in an alphabet rhyme: 'X was
expensive, and so became poor'. But the editing for the early part of
the Dictionary was done about a hundred years ago now; and in the
absence of any further comments from the Supplements, we may
surely consider, in this and several other instances, that this part of
the Regency legacy is now null and void.

In Jane Austen's day, *grateful* regularly bore the sense of 'gratifying'. Elizabeth Bennet persuades her friend Charlotte Lucas that
Charlotte's marriage is 'highly *grateful*' to her (*Pride and Prejudice*, ch.
22). The word was still being used vestigially in this sense at the end
of the nineteenth century. Professor Collinson, in his *Contemporary
English*,[3] reviewing the advertising slogans of his youth, recalls
'Epps' Cocoa, *grateful* and comforting'. But *grateful* and *comforting*, he
tells us, were rumoured to be the names of Epps's two daughters.
Such witticism suggests that the word *grateful* had become obsolescent in contexts where there was no suggestion of thankfulness for
favours received.

What we can observe at times (*pace* some semantic theorists) is a
kind of semantic jockeying for position. While the word *address*, for
example, is needed to describe a person's bearing, as when in *Pride
and Prejudice* (ch. 30) someone is described as 'in person and *address*
most truly the gentleman', the noun is not fully appropriated to the
meaning of an inscription on letters, for which, in the early
nineteenth century, a regular word was *direction*. When Marianne
Dashwood wrote a note to her lover Willoughby, the letter 'was
sealed and *directed* with eager rapidity. Elinor thought she could
distinguish a large W. in the *direction*' (*Sense and Sensibility*, ch. 26).

---

[2] The danger of categorizing a word as obsolete is well seen in H.C.
Wyld's *The Universal Dictionary of the English Language* (1932), where the
word *lollipop* is described as a 'childish word, now hardly in actual use
among any class of speakers in England'!

[3] W.E. Collinson, *Contemporary English: a Personal Speech Record* (Leipzig
and Berlin, 1927), p. 65.

Still, in 1878, Disraeli, a great connoisseur of archaism, could write: 'I'm glad to *direct* this to Melbury. . . . If Monty sees the *direction* he will begin to sigh' (*Letters*, II.156).[4] It seems odd to us, too, that at one point in Jane Austen's novel Emma could look 'unconscious' as well as 'innocent' (*Emma*, ch. 23); but as long as *conscious* carries the eighteenth-century meaning of 'in the know' (to quote Susie Tucker again), *unconscious* still cannot exclusively mean 'not in possession of one's senses'. In this particular context, for example, Emma is merely unembarrassed. We might bear in mind here that, when Louisa Musgrove falls on the Cobb at Lyme Regis, she is taken up, not *unconscious*, but *insensible*. As late as 1860, Thomas Hughes could write of 'that fearless *unconsciousness* which looks out from pure hearts' (*Tom Brown at Oxford*, ch. 26). Again, a word like *genius* could still be used by Jane Austen for qualities of mind that were in no way exceptional or outstanding, as when Aunt Norris accuses Fanny Price of showing a 'great want of *genius*' in her lessons (*Mansfield Park*, ch. 2). Among other things, this left the word *intelligence* more unrestricted than it is apt to be today; so that, when Mr Knightley in *Emma* (ch. 41) notices 'symptoms of *intelligence*' between Jane Fairfax and Frank Churchill, he is not playing the part of a sarcastic schoolmaster, as we might think, but merely noting signs of mutual understanding. It is a meaning, according to the *OED* (*intelligence* 5), that is rare or obsolete now.

A *position*, for Jane Austen, could mean something that one posits, or what we should call a proposition: 'Catherine's feelings contradicted almost every *position* her mother advanced' (*Northanger Abbey*, ch. 29). We find Disraeli still using the word thus in his *Reminiscences* in the 1860s:[5] 'But this does not affect my *position* that it is difficult if not impossible to ruin a family well rooted in the land' (p. 135). It is tempting, but it would probably be wrong, to feel that this meaning has been eclipsed by important mid- and late-Victorian developments of this word *position*. I am thinking particularly of *OED* sense 9b 'place in the social scale' and sense 9c 'an official situation, place, or employment'. The former sense dates from 1865 in the Dictionary, and the latter from 1890. We find Mrs Gaskell using the word with inverted commas, evidently as something new,

---

[4] The Marquis of Zetland (ed.), *Letters of Disraeli to Lady Bradford and Lady Chesterfield*, 2 vols. (London, 1929).

[5] Benjamin Disraeli, *Reminiscences*, ed. Helen and Marvin Swartz (London, 1975).

in the sixties: 'Their "position"—poor as the Hamleys might be—was far higher than his own in the county' (*Wives and Daughters*, ch. 31). In sense 9c the word is a rather snobbish replacement for *situation*, which had done duty in such contexts all the century hitherto. That Victorian sociologist, Richard Jefferies, takes note of the new development in *Hodge and His Masters* (1880) as he describes the farmers' daughters turning their backs on young farmers and preferring 'a banker's clerk at least—nothing could be thought of under a clerk in the local banks; of course, his salary was not high, but then his "position"' (ch. 10). The word comes so naturally to us in this sense that the more or less equivalent use of *situation* in Jane Austen now sounds odd: 'From *situation* Mrs Clay was . . . a very unequal, and in her character a very dangerous companion' (*Persuasion*, ch. 2).

When we talk of personal qualities, we tend now to mean qualities of the personality; whereas at the beginning of the last century, the suggestions of *person* and *personal* were often physical, concerning the body. Thus, when in *Pendennis* (I, ch. 9) the elderly Dr Portman, Vicar of Clavering, sees the beautiful actress Miss Fotheringay, he exclaims 'I must say, Major, she is endowed with very considerable *personal* attractions'. The heroine's rival, Miss Ingram, we are told in *Jane Eyre* (ch. 18) 'had a fine *person*'; we should be more likely to say 'was a fine person', and go on to delineate her character. Only the adjective *personable* retains today the connection with appearance. The same physical meaning had formerly occurred with the adverb also; thus, though Emma Woodhouse is beautiful, Mr Knightley does not 'think her *personally* vain' (*Emma*, ch. 5), that is, vain as to her beauty. A much more likely modern sentence, with a quite different meaning, would be 'Personally, I do not think her vain'; but this use of *personally*, meaning 'so far as I personally am concerned', was not available to Jane Austen. It is a Victorian innovation in our language, first illustrated in the OED from Macaulay. We find an elderly character laughing at the new idiom in Mrs Gaskell's *North and South* (1855):

> 'Papa, I do think Mr Thornton a very remarkable man; but personally, I don't like him at all.' 'And I do!' said her father, laughing. '*Personally*, as you call it, and all.'   (ch. 11)

Two words destined for growth and increased currency as the century proceeded were *development* and *organization*. From its etymology, the verb *develop* has the meaning of 'to unfurl, unroll, what is rolled up'. In a direct figurative extension of this sense, Jane Austen contrasts Mrs Bennet, in *Pride and Prejudice*, with her husband:

> The experience of three and thirty years had been insufficient to make his wife understand his character. *Her* mind was less difficult to *develope* [*sic*]. (ch. 1)

Similarly Disraeli, in *Coningsby* (III, ch. 3) describes young men making merry: 'their boyish feelings, and still latent boyish character, *developed* with their reminiscences'. The noun *development* bore the same idea of revelation rather than the later meaning of growth:

> It required some time to make Madame Colonna comprehend the nature of his communication. All Rigby's diplomatic skill was expended in the gradual *development*. When it was once fairly put before her, the effect was appalling. (V, ch. 6)

The rather different idea of causing to grow what exists in the germ (*OED develop* 6) was much in vogue at the mid-century; witness the Dictionary's 1866 quotation: 'They grow, or in modern phraseology, they are developed'. Both the verb, and especially the noun, became closely identified with theories of *evolution*—the etymological idea, of unrolling, unfurling, is common to both words, and there is some cross-referencing in the Dictionary. A nice instance of the new, and more organic, meaning occurs when the young scientist Roger Hamley, in *Wives and Daughters* (ch. 10), is described as avoiding walking unnecessarily on any plant: 'Who knew what long-sought growth or insect might *develop* in that which now appeared insignificant?'

The predominantly bureaucratic modern meaning of the word *organization*, 'an organized body, system or society' (*OED* sense 2c), is late in its arrival into English. The word was used originally to describe the human, or any other, living organism. Victorian novelists like Dickens and Henry James, therefore, are fully justified etymologically, though perhaps not immediately understood today, when they refer, in effect, to a human being as an *organization:* 'Waldershore was one of those vivid and brilliant *organizations* which exercise a peculiarly attractive influence on youth' (Disraeli, *Endymion*, ch. 22). Henry James appears to revel in the word (though perhaps he senses that it is already obsolescent) to describe the totality of the intellectual and sentient being that is Isabel Archer: 'One should be ... conscious of a fine *organization* (she could not help knowing her *organization* was fine).' (*The Portrait of a Lady*, ch. 6). Modern bureaucratic developments would appear to have completely ousted this meaning.

A third word destined for increased use, with the loss of some earlier meanings, was *appointment*, though in this case the predominant modern meaning of an assignation, or an arrangement for meeting, is early in the language. What we have lost, for the most part, is the theological overtones of the word, which still throve at the beginning of the nineteenth century. If called upon, we should probably substitute *dispensation* in a phrase like Jane Austen's 'the merciful *appointment* of Providence' (*Mansfield Park*, ch. 47). But the word *appointment* on its own was enough to suggest Divine intervention at this time: Mrs Smith, in *Persuasion* (ch. 17), though a sad cripple, had elasticity of spirits which 'by a merciful *appointment*' seemed 'designed to counterbalance almost every other want'. Probably the usage continued longest with the more extreme sects. The ferociously puritanical Mrs Clennam, in *Little Dorrit* (11, ch. 30), says to an adversary: 'It may seem so, to such as you who know no righteousness, and no *appointment* except Satan's.'

There is one word, eminently characteristic of the first half of the nineteenth century, which is of special interest in so far as it reflects the intense religious feeling of the time. This is *serious*, meaning 'earnest about the things of religion' (*OED* sense 2), first illustrated in the Dictionary from 1796. Jane Austen describes Mr Elliot, in *Persuasion*, as having been 'careless on all *serious* matters.... How could it ever be ascertained that his mind was truly cleansed?' (ch. 17). Henry Kingsley tells us that 'A majority of young fellows at the University deceive their parents, especially if they come of *serious* houses' (*Ravenshoe*, ch. 8). In practice, the word *serious* often meant 'of the evangelical persuasion'. In *The Newcomes*, Thackeray describes a typical *serious* establishment at Clapham, where even 'the lodge-keeper was *serious*, and a clerk at a neighbouring chapel' (I, ch. 2). The word in this sense is much less common in the second half of the century; it seems to have been already going out of fashion when Thomas Hughes wrote the preface to his sixth (1858) edition of *Tom Brown's School Days:* 'But this boyishness in the highest sense is not incompatible with *seriousness*, or *earnestness*, if you like the word better.' A footnote directs us to the source of this emendation: 'To him [Arnold] and his admirers we owe the substitution of the word *earnest* for its predecessor *serious*.' Presumably *serious* as an adjective had become somewhat institutionalized, and too closely associated with the evangelical movement.

Besides meaning 'inquisitive', the word *curious* also formerly had the meaning of 'taking the interest of a connoisseur'. Jane Austen describes a certain Lord Bolton as being 'particularly *curious* in his pigs, has had pigstyes of a most elegant construction built for them'.[6] In *Ravenshoe* Lord Ascot, a follower of cockfighting, is described, ironically, as 'very *curious* in his poultry' (ch. 5). Something approaching this usage is to be found when the word is used as late as 1879 by Disraeli in one of his letters[7], when he describes a meal with the future Edward VII: 'a first-rate dinner which even Prince Hal, very *curious* in such matters, noticed with much praise'. *Great* is another word that underwent some change in the nineteenth century. The *OED* informs us that, if used with reference to physical stature and size, *great* now expresses some feeling such as surprise, contempt, or admiration (sense 6). We should now often substitute more neutral adjectives like *large* or *big*; as for instance when Jane Austen writes that Mr Elton was 'the adoration of all the teachers and *great* girls in the school' (*Emma*, ch. 17). Perhaps Trollope would have us see the elderly Mr Harding recalling the language of his youth when he says to his little granddaughter, 'When Posy is a *great* girl she can go to the cathedral every day' (*Last Chronicle of Barset*, ch. 49). The word *rate* tends now to be used of solid valuations of money and of speed. It is hardly now found of more abstract evaluations, as in Jane Austen's 'the children . . . were talked to and admired amid the usual *rate* of conversation' (*Emma*, ch. 26). The usage survives into the mid-century: 'Different as were their dispositions and the *rate* of their abilities, their political opinions were the same' (*Coningsby*, VI, ch. 3).

These are slight differences in significance, however; it is not often that, when reading Victorian novels, we come upon a meaning that is so unfamiliar as to send us to the dictionary. But such a word is *notable* in the sense (*OED* 4b) 'of women: capable, bustling, industrious in household management'. The *OED* describes this sense as in common use from *c*. 1750, but now 'somewhat rare'; and it notes that in this sense the word seems to have been pronounced with a short 'o'. It is a favourite, predictably, with Mrs Gaskell: 'the little, *notable-looking* brown hands'; 'Mary has infected me with her *notability*, and I'm going to work mamma a footstool' (*Wives and Daughters*, chs. 53,

---

[6] R.W. Chapman, *Jane Austen's Letters*, 2 vols. (Oxford, 1932), p. 36.
[7] *Letters of Disraeli*, II. 260.

54). A now unfamiliar word that was very much of the first half of the century is *knowing* in the sense of 'smart' or, as the OED puts it, 'knowing "what is what" in fashion, dress and the like'. Jane Austen speaks of young men driving about town 'in very *knowing* gigs' (*Sense and Sensibility*, ch. 19); and at Rugby, Tom Brown thought his cap 'a very *knowing* affair' (*Tom Brown's School Days*, ch. 5). *Outcry*, meaning an 'auction sale', is also likely to be unfamiliar, as when Dobbin, in *Vanity Fair* (ch. 38), sold poor quality wine 'at public *outcry*, at an enormous loss to himself'. The word *illustration* in the sense of distinction, or an example, means or cause of distinction, is not uncommon in the first half of the century: 'His dinners were celebrated at least for their guests. Great intellectual *illustrations* were found there, blended with rank and high station' (Disraeli, *Coningsby*, I, ch. 5).

Rather old-fashioned novels, such as Mrs Gaskell's *Wives and Daughters*, or those written by authors very conscious of a tradition of novel-writing, such as Henry James's *The Portrait of a Lady*, are apt to use more traditional vocabulary. *Wives and Daughters* must have been written with Jane Austen strongly in mind. There is much talk of *attachments* and *engagements* to indicate stages of a love-affair; though, as in Jane Austen, *to be engaged* might merely mean to be booked for a dance (ch. 25). People go *a-shopping* (ch. 20), as they had done in Fanny Burney's *Evelina*. Using Austenian language, Mrs Gaskell describes a visit to local nobility as 'a *variety*', or, as we should say, 'a change' (ch. 45); and speaks of the duress under which her heroine lives at one period as 'the *stretch* of restraint' (ch. 48). Ladies wear *gowns* or *frocks*, but not *dresses*; these last being a late-comer into English—the Dictionary adds, almost as an afterthought (*dress* 2b) 'Mod. She has had a new silk dress for the occasion'. There is plenty of evidence that, down to the beginning of this century, the word *dress* in this sense was considered (in modern parlance) non-U. *Wives and Daughters* is set a generation before its composition in the sixties. Mrs Gaskell takes us back to a time when there were still a few sedan chairs, when railways had only just begun, and there were no gummed envelopes; all which changes she mentions. The language reinforces the feeling of a safe, old-fashioned story, in the reading of which we must forgo, as the Victorian reader did, all but the most innocent interpretations of phrases like 'carrying on some underhand intercourse' (ch. 42) or 'going and making love to this girl, that day he left' (ch. 39), or (an old-fashioned speaker) 'he went in "promiscuous"', i.e. without ceremony (ch. 12). *Passionateness* is used of 'the passions' generally, and not confined, as the word *passion* often is today, to one: the heroine, in *Wives and Daughters* (ch. 29), kisses her father 'in a sad *passionateness* of affection'. An innovation is the word *demonstrative*, which in the nineteenth century developed the new meaning of 'given to outward expression of the feelings'. Mrs Gaskell describes the hero's brother as 'almost as *demonstrative* as a girl' (ch. 4). We find Charles Kingsley, in *Two Years Ago* (1857) writing: 'though his feelings were not *"demonstrative"*, as fine ladies say nowadays' (ch. 1). It is a word that Jane Austen would have liked.

Henry James, also, relied on the occasional old-fashioned expression or nuance of meaning to promote the strong feeling one has, in reading, for example, *The Portrait of a Lady* (1881), that one is in good hands. Characters 'look *conscious*' (ch. 44), as they do in Richardson. The heroine fears 'the chance of inflicting a *sensible* injury' upon another person (ch. 12). This last is *OED sensible* sense 6, marked as obsolete by the Dictionary, and meaning 'acutely felt'. When Isabel Archer explains to her cousin that her friend Henrietta had no *'interested* views' (ch. 10) in trying to attract him, the collocation places James in the great tradition of English novelists, recalling Richardson and Jane Austen. *Interested* in the sense of 'self-seeking, self-interested, biassed', as when Thackeray (*The Newcomes*, II, ch. 21) writes of *'interested* marriages' which have wretched consequences, is a meaning almost lost to us, and it must have been archaic in 1881. A rearguard action is still being fought over the last remnant of this once frequent meaning: the word *disinterested*; which, however, is rapidly ceasing to mean 'unbiassed' and meaning 'apathetic'. *View* in the sense of 'aim' rather than the modern 'opinion' is also of the eighteenth century. Lord Warburton (and who more appropriately?) uses a favourite, if rather colloquial, word of Jane Austen's to describe a definite and necessary sacrifice:

> 'If you are mistaken, Miss Archer, let me lose all I possess!'
> She wondered whether he meant this for a reminder that he was rich, and, in the instant, felt sure that he did not. He was *sinking* that, as he would have said himself.   (ch. 12)

We are reminded of John Thorpe's exaggerated account to General Tilney of the Morland family's fortune: 'by trebling [Mr Morland's] private fortune, bestowing a rich aunt, and *sinking* half the children, he was able to represent the whole family ... in a most respectable light' (*Northanger Abbey*, ch. 30). James can still, of course, use *grateful* in the sense of 'gratifying' ('this was *grateful* to her pride', ch. 21); and *address*, meaning 'bearing in conversation', as when Lord Warburton advanced 'with his English *address*, in which a vague shyness seemed to offer itself as an element of good breeding' (ch. 46). The word *branch* used without further qualification in the general meaning of a department is a favourite of Jane Austen's, and survives in free use with James:

> 'We have gymnastics,' the Italian visitor ventured to remark. 'But not dangerous.'
> 'I hope not. Is that your *branch*?'   (ch. 22)

Again, we have to disabuse our minds of recent suggestions with certain words and phrases. Passion is not exclusively sexual: Isabel Archer is capable of '*passionate* humility' (ch. 6); nor must we augur the inevitable, as we should today, when Henrietta Stackpole and Mr Bantling led a life in Paris 'of great intimacy'; 'really in a manner quite lived together' (ch. 20). When Lord Warburton is 'in the act of making love to a young lady' (ch. 12), James merely means paying his addresses to her.

A new word that James rather rejoices in is *personage*. Until the nineteenth century, the *OED* tells us, this word was always combined with *great* or the like qualification; James savours its use in solitary splendour:

> The intimation that she was admired by a '*personage*' struck her. . . . She had never known a personage before; there were no personages in her native land.   (ch.12)

Turning from vocabulary to grammar and idiom, we can observe that it is phrasal verbs, those combinations of verb and particle so very essential to English, which change with most rapidity over the decades. In Jane Austen's time, fine weather *turned off*, unsatisfactory servants were *turned away*, and Catherine Morland is overjoyed that 'with all the chances against her of house, hall, park, court, and cottage, Northanger *turned up* an Abbey'. Such usage, like many another idiosyncratic collocation of the Regency period, does not die out immediately. In *Bleak House* (ch. 37) Dickens talks of 'the perfect ease of manner with which [Skimpole] *put* the money *up* again'. This does not mean, as it would now, that he made a second bet; it is the eighteenth-century, and Regency, use of *put up*, meaning 'put away'. Today, we *come across* things rather than letting them *come across* us.

This latter usage for 'to cross one's mind' is found in Richardson and Jane Austen, and carries on to the mid–Victorian period; as when, in *Tom Brown at Oxford*, the hero was 'silent and absent' (we should say 'absent-minded') as the 'remembrance of the ... scene at the public-house ... *came across* him' (ch. 26). There are many slight differences. Mrs Gibson, in *Wives and Daughters* (ch. 35), went into her husband's surgery and *looked out* (where we should say 'looked up') the name of a disease. Reassuring a patient, Dr Gibson says 'We'll soon *bring* you *about*', i.e. cure you (ch. 29). From an expression like 'I don't *set* myself *up* as a saint' (*Wives and Daughters*, ch. 44) comes *set up*, meaning 'high-minded, conceited': 'Let us hear how you behaved among the great folks. You must not be *set up* with all their attention' (ch. 58). Usage varies with the ensuing particle both ways: 'She has given the hotel clerk a *dressing*' (*Portrait of a Lady*, ch. 1) seems to demand nowadays the additional particle *down*; whereas with Mrs Gaskell's *bedding-out* plants (*Wives and Daughters*, ch. 1) the particle now seems redundant.

Usage in regard to the transitivity and intransitivity of verbs fluctuates considerably. In the language of the upper classes intransitive verbs are probably more common, because a certain exclusiveness is suggested, along with an elegant brevity in some instances, by the omission of the object. Expressions like 'Did you *find*?' (the fox), 'You don't *preserve*' (game), and 'I must *show*' (myself in public) speak for themselves. There are many other instances: 'I found my pupil sufficiently docile, though disinclined to *apply*' (*Jane Eyre*, ch. 11). 'Only send us a card, "*to remind*"' (*Tom Brown at Oxford*, ch. 10). 'Is he going to *offer*?' thought she, with a sudden palpitation' (*Wives and Daughters*, ch. 10); and a variant of the same, 'Is it settled?' she asked, 'Has he *popped*?' (*Last Chronicle of Barset*, ch. 7). Alongside all this, certain verbs occur in unfamiliar transitive use. Jane Austen and Scott had both used *recover* and *participate* with no preposition intervening before the object, and with the former verb this usage continues. In his *Reminiscences*,[8] Disraeli mentions an envious prelate who 'never *recovered* the appointment of Dr Thomson to York'. *Hope* occurs transitively in Jane Austen ('to submit quietly and *hope* the best', *Mansfield Park*, ch. 36); and the usage is to be found in early Victorian English: 'Everything might still be *hoped* from his youth' (*Pendennis*, II, ch. 14). *To joke* and the colloquial equivalent *to lark* could both be transitive verbs: 'The young fellows ... gave parties ... partly to *joke* him and partly to do him honour' (*Pendennis*, I, ch.

[8] *Reminiscences*, p. 111.

21); 'playing leap-frog and *larking* one another' (*Tom Brown at Oxford*, ch. 24).

With tenses of the verb, it is noticeable that the preterite is frequent where we now expect a perfect, particularly the perfect of experience, in a sentence like 'I have never been to Spain'. The simple past tense is now rare in such contexts, but was commoner in the nineteenth century:

'*Were you* ever at a county fair?'
'*I never was* at one.'   (Kingsley, *Yeast*, ch. 4)

The hotel seems comfortable. I never *was* in it before.
                                           (*The Newcomes*, I, ch. 12)

If the perfect tense of finite verbs is rather less common, however, the past infinitive, also with *have*, is more frequent. This is a legacy from the previous century, when writers like Fanny Burney, for example, regularly indicated an abortive hope, aim, or expectation, or any possibility not realized, with the perfect infinitive. Writers of refined narratives like Mrs Gaskell are rather fond of retaining the perfect infinitive in such contexts, for their socially acceptable characters:

I was going *to have asked* for a longer visit the next time you came.
                                           (*Wives and Daughters*, ch. 7)

I wanted *to have come* early.   (ch. 26)

I quite expected *to have seen* Mr Thornton.
                                           (*North and South*, ch. 37)

With usage in regard to expanded tenses, the reader is often surprised, in reading Victorian novels, as in Jane Austen, when they are avoided; particularly, for example, with questions in the present tense:

'*Do you dine* at home, Philip?' his father asks.
'*Do you*, sir? I will if you do.'   (Thackeray, *Philip*, I, ch. 10)

The usage with *do* here would now of course be thought more appropriate to habitual action. The expanded tenses, however, are much in evidence; even the expansion of the verb *to be*, which we think of as recent: 'The daughter couldn't always, you see, be *being* ill' (Thackeray, *Roundabout Papers*, 'On a Medal of George the Fourth'); 'You are always *being* wrong' (*Last Chronicle of Barset*, ch. 47). But Jespersen is doubtless right to say that such usage is rare in the first half of the century.[9]

As to auxiliary verbs, there has been some change since the time of Jane Austen in the use of *must have*. We now use *must have* to express supposition or certainty about the past: 'you *must have* been a beautiful baby' is a present-day assertion about past glory! In Jane Austen's novels, and frequently in early Victorian English, *must have* relates wholly to past time, indicating necessity in the past:

> If the secret I had to keep had been mine, I *must have* confided it to Ada.　　　　　　　　　　　　　　　　　　(*Bleak House*, ch. 37)

> He *must have* submitted to be told that he was a fiend. . . . But he would have been called upon for no further mental effort.
> (*The Way We Live Now*, ch. 26)

Might sometimes occurs, in a manner that the *OED* states is rare now, in place of modern *may have*. The *OED* (*may* v. 5c) commends the current form as being more logical, 'as the subjective possibility is a matter of the speaker's present':

> Clive turned very red, and perhaps a faint blush *might appear* on Barnes's pallid countenance.　　　　(*The Newcomes*, I, ch. 14)

> So, probably, 200 and 202 in Curzon Street *might know* what was going on.　　　　　　　　　　　　　　　(*Vanity Fair*, ch. 37)

Abstract nouns that are normally singular with us, are sometimes found in the plural, after an earlier mode:

> I was her confidant in her *loves* with poor Mr Kirkpatrick.
> (*Wives and Daughters*, ch. 8)

> Molly could not help trying to piece these strange facts together by *imaginations* of her own.　　　　　　　　　　　　　(ch. 46)

A corollary of this is that, as often in the previous century, an abstract noun could be preceded by an indefinite article, with the meaning 'an

[9] Otto Jespersen, *A Modern English Grammar* (London, 1961), Part IV, p. 225.

act of, instance of (the quality in question)': 'after a generous and manly *conduct*' (*Pendennis*, II, ch. 19). This, however, is rare in Victorian novels; as is the normally eighteenth-century occurrence of a singular noun after the phrase 'series of': 'To me he has been the last and worst of a long series of . . . undeserved *misfortune*' (*The Way We Live Now*, ch. 91).

A regular idiom, in the first half of the century, was 'change of air and scene', with no indefinite article: 'I wonder if she wants *change of air*' (*Wives and Daughters*, ch. 28). It is the definite article that is omitted, to our ears, from *out of window*: 'Mr Guppy has been lolling *out of window* all morning' (*Bleak House*, ch. 20); while it seems to us to have been unnecessarily included in expressions like 'master of *the* ceremonies' (Kingsley, *Glaucus*, 1st edition, p. 119)—but this had been the regular Bath usage. Referring to women as 'the sex' is eighteenth-century and Regency usage, and comes naturally from Mr Turveydrop in *Bleak House* (ch. 23): 'Again *the sex* stimulates us, and rewards us, by the condescension of its lovely presence.' The definite article with diseases was commoner than now; it was not until the very end of the century that such a phrase as *the rheumatism* was felt to be old-fashioned and bucolic. Down to at least 1850, it was usual to include the article with *The Regent's Park* and *The Paddington Station*; and the season of Christmas was signalized by an article, as it still is dialectally: 'I would fain have returned home earlier that we might have been at Lowick for *the Christmas*' (*Middlemarch*, ch. 20).

Prepositional usage that differs from ours is the fairly common 'interested *about*' for 'interested *in*', and 'made a fuss *with*' for 'made a fuss *of*': 'He seemed very much *interested about* Mr Campion's cab and horse' (*Pendennis*, II, ch. 9); 'a good deal of *fuss* had been made *with* him by certain leading politicians' (*The Way We Live Now*, ch. 69). *From* in the sense of 'away from' is regular usage in 'from home': 'My father is annoyed enough about my going *from home* so often' (*Wives and Daughters*, ch. 29). A similar crispness is conferred by the elliptical partitive 'of all things', for 'most of all things': 'There was to be "Don Giovanni", which he admired *of all things*' (*Pendennis*, I, ch. 20). It was not substandard, well into the nineteenth century, to introduce the idea of a habitual time of day with *of*: 'He used to take him out *of* mornings' (*Vanity Fair*, ch. 37); 'Gallant young fellows . . . with whom he drank . . . and beat the town *of* a night' (*Pendennis*, I, ch. 20). We should now consider it redundant to add an extra *for* after *think* in 'Matrimony's not so bad as you think *for*' (*Wives and Daughters*, ch. 46); but this was a regular idiom. On the other hand, we should probably now consider an additional *to* essential in contexts like this: 'I haven't opened a book yet, and don't *mean*' (*Tom Brown at Oxford*, ch. 10); 'You cannot; you *ought* not' (*Jane Eyre*, ch. 34). The *OED* describes the additional *to* we feel we need here (*to* 21) as 'rare before the nineteenth century; now a frequent colloquialism'. The upper classes seemed particularly reluctant to end their sentences with any sort of preposition; in other contexts, too, they showed that eighteenth-century grammarians' inhibitions about ending sentences thus were still influential: 'Good heavens! Lufton, for what do you take them?' (*Framley Parsonage*, ch. 31); 'Good heavens, Touchett!' cried Lord Warburton, angrily, 'For what do you take me?' (*The Portrait of a Lady*, ch. 39).

VII

The Irreconcilable Dimensions of Faulkner's 'As I Lay Dying'

C.H. PEAKE

Few critics have been misled by Faulkner's much-quoted statement about *As I Lay Dying*:

> I simply imagined a group of people and subjected them to the simple universal natural catastrophes, which are flood and fire, with a simple natural motive to give direction to their progress.[1]

The reiteration smacks of tongue-in-cheek; the fire in the novel is by no means a natural catastrophe; there is no single motive; and, in any case, Faulkner carefully ascribes simplicity only to the ingredients of the story, not to his handling of it. The fundamental complexity is suggested even by critics' attempts to categorize the novel: it has been variously labelled an odyssey, a mock-epic, a legend, a folk-tale, a fable, and an allegory, while its tone has been called tragic, heroic, tragicomic, comic, farcical, cynical, grotesque, and macabre, usually with an antithetical pairing of some of these terms:

> tragedy and comedy, terror and farce, are perpetually juxtaposed and reconciled in terms of the frontier-peasant tradition of humorous realism.[2]

However, the complexity does not arise from the mere presence of such contrasted elements—plenty of novels and plays have a similar mixture—but from the manner of their juxtaposition, a manner which stresses incompatibility rather than reconciliation.

To begin with, the form seems at odds with the story. Nothing could seem less suitable for the narrative of a journey made in the face

---

[1] Jean Stein, 'William Faulkner: An Interview', *Paris Review* (Spring 1956). Reprinted in *William Faulkner: Three Decades of Criticism*, ed. Frederick J. Hoffman and Olga W. Vickery (East Lancing, 1960), p. 73.

[2] Michael Millgate, *William Faulkner*, Writers and Critics (Edinburgh and London, 1961), p. 39.

of 'universal natural catastrophes' than interior monologue, a form which implies that the significant events occur in the mind rather than in the physical world. Moreover, Faulkner has devised an extraordinary specimen of that form with fifty-nine separate monologues distributed among fifteen separate characters, some of them involved in the action only briefly and in passing. Of the monologuizing characters only two are significantly self-aware and articulate, Darl and Addie: the two men most responsible for the completion of the journey are poorly represented, Jewel by a single passage prior to his mother's death and Anse by three short passages all before the crossing of the flooded river: the crucial scenes of the death of Addie and the completion of her coffin are both presented through the interior monologues of Darl who is miles away at the time, so that, instead of knowledge of what happens at the Bundrens, the reader is offered only what Darl imagines is happening: and, of course, the one interior monologue from Addie comes apparently when her body, already stinking in its coffin, has been rescued from the river. Finally, the monologues vary extravagantly in style, not merely from person to person, but within a single passage, leaping from the barely articulate to the rhetorical and symbolic:

> I said You don't know what worry is. I don't know what it is. I don't know whether I am worrying or not. Whether I can or not. I don't know whether I can cry or not. I don't know whether I have tried to or not. I feel like a wet seed wild in the hot blind earth (p. 58).[3]

Discrepancies between content and form are complicated by multiple incongruities within the form.

The story itself is equally riddled with incongruities. According to Anse, the journey is motivated by the need to honour Addie's wish to be buried at Jefferson and for all her family to take part in that posthumous fulfilment. But of those who combine to honour the wish, Anse is driven by the desire to get some false teeth in town, Dewey Dell by the hope of obtaining an abortifacient, and Vardaman by the dream of seeing a toy train in a shopwindow. Cash is governed mainly by pride of workmanship in the coffin, the planks of which he has repeatedly held up for his dying mother's inspection;

[3] All page-references are to the edition published by Chatto and Windus (London, 1952; first published 1935).

Jewel violently throws the coffin about regardless of its contents; Vardaman drills holes in the coffin-lid and in doing so drills holes into the face of the corpse. The only journeyer who shows respect for the dead body, Darl, tries to prevent the completion of the journey, and, in consequence, is viciously assaulted by his family, and committed to an asylum. Even Addie's request to be buried at Jefferson is anything but simply motivated: it is a kind of revenge on her husband, and a cleaning away of her life with her family as being no more than 'getting ready to stay dead' (p. 164).

The peculiarities of the novel reflect a peculiarity in the object about which the action turns—Addie Bundren's coffin. Cash has constructed it in the traditional shape, widest at the shoulders and tapering towards the feet, but because the women want to bury Addie in her full-skirted wedding-dress, they lay her in the coffin upside-down. Consequently, as Cash repeatedly complains, 'It won't balance' (p. 87). The inverted body and the unbalanced coffin together form a symbol of the whole novel where nothing seems to be as it should be or as one might have expected it to be.

But the discrepancies are certainly not random: they may be unreconciled, but they are all of a kind, and combine in an integrated fictional pattern. They are rooted in conflicts which give rise to the action and shape its developments, but, if one wished to represent these conflicts diagrammatically, a straight line with deflections or with arrows pointing in opposite directions would not do: the appropriate diagram would have to be L-shaped with one arrow pointing vertically and the other horizontally, because the clashes are not between human purpose and natural obstacles, nor between diametrically opposed wills, but between ways of seeing and being which exist on different planes, in different dimensions. That Faulkner had some such diagram in mind is suggested by the patterned incompatibles of his novel and confirmed by his repeated use, in crucial passages throughout the novel, of images where one existence or attitude is explicitly set at right-angles to another.

The main pairs of these dimensionally contrasted forces can be labelled inertia and movement, words and doing, rigidity and fluidity, space and time: but I don't wish to insist on the terms themselves; they serve only as a framework on which to disentangle the persistent, intricate, and significant pattern which dominates *As I Lay Dying*.

The *inertia-movement* clash is most memorably expressed in and by Anse Bundren, who hasn't visited the town for twelve years. In

Anse's own eyes, he is the most 'misfortunate' of men, and he attributes his misfortunes to the road that has been built past his house: it is the road, he believes, which took his sons to work away from home and left him short-handed, and it is the road which is responsible for his wife's sickness, since she would have been all right if it hadn't been that the road brought the doctor who pronounced her sick. Bad luck travels along the road: even the rainstorm that causes the flood finds its way to Anse's door by the road:

> A-laying there, right up to my door, where every bad luck that comes and goes is bound to find it. I told Addie it wasn't any luck living on a road when it come by here, and she said, for the world like a woman, 'Get up and move, then.' But I told her it wasn't no luck in it, because the Lord put roads for travelling: why He laid them down flat on the earth. When He aims for something to be always a-moving, He makes it long ways, like a road or a horse or a wagon, but when He aims for something to stay put, He makes it up-and-down ways, like a tree or a man.... [I]t's always men can't rest till they gets the house set where everybody that passes in a wagon can spit in the doorway, keeping the folks restless and wanting to get up and go somewheres else when He aimed for them to stay put like a tree or a stand of corn. Because if He'd a aimed for man to be always a-moving and going somewheres else, wouldn't He a put him longways on his belly, like a snake? It stands to reason He would (pp. 30–1).

The clash between Anse's vertical inertia and Addie's horizontal movement, figured here in the right-angled image, is the origin of the whole action of the novel.

Anse returns to the image to explain Darl's strangeness:

> ... he was all right at first, with his eyes full of the land, because the land laid up-and-down ways then; it wasn't till that ere road come and switched the land around longways and his eyes still full of the land, that they begun to threaten me out of him, trying to short-hand me with the law (p. 31).

For Anse, it is the longways road which has led to the loss of his wife and, ironically, it is that bereavement which sends him out travelling the road. Initially, however, Addie's death deprives him of the horizontal force on which he depends for movement, a deprivation expressed again in a right-angled image when Vern Tull finds him

standing there like a scarecrow, like he was a steer standing
knee-deep in a pond and somebody come by and set the pond up
on edge and he ain't missed it yet (p. 65).

Addie has been the source of all movement for Anse. Tull says of
her,

> 'She kept him at work for thirty-odd years. I reckon she is tired'
> (p. 28),

to which Kate prophetically adds that, if his wife dies, Anse will 'get
another one before cotton-picking' (p. 28).

At one level, Addie's revenge on Anse is to exact the promise to
bury her at Jefferson, so that, after her death, he will be obliged to
move. The revenge misfires largely because she has not recognized
the completeness of Anse's inertia, for inertia is not merely immobility: it is what keeps an object moving after the initial source of
movement has ceased. Once Anse has been set in motion, it is easier
for him to keep moving than to stop or return. Samson makes the
point explicitly:

> I notice how it takes a lazy man, a man that hates moving, to get
> set on moving once he does get started off, the same as he was set
> on staying still, like it ain't the moving he hates so much as the
> starting and the stopping. And like he would be kind of proud of
> whatever come up to make the moving or the setting still look
> hard (p. 101).

Anse's moving only looks hard; he depends on others for all the
effort. He is not involved in the struggle to cross the ford or to rescue
the coffin from the fire. It is only when events can be used to move
him towards some goal of his own that he appears to take action, as
when he trades Jewel's horse and Cash's money for mules to replace
those he has lost. Otherwise Anse rides on the backs of others, his
inertia so accepted by them that they take the demands on them as
inescapable: Tull speaks for others when he says to himself, 'Like
most folks around here, I done help him so much already I can't quit
now' (p. 28), and Uncle Billy believes that the Lord's assistance will
be equally forthcoming for Anse:

> 'I reckon He's like everybody else around here. . . . He's done it
> so long now He can't quit' (p. 81).

In this way Anse's inertia is not an obstacle to movement. It is neither resistant nor opposed to Addie's wish to be buried in Jefferson, because it operates in a different dimension: it makes use of movement originated and sustained by others to be swept effortlessly towards its own ends—in Anse's case, a set of teeth and a new wife.

The *words-doing* discrepancy is, as it were, an internal equivalent to inertia and movement, because in the mind of Addie, who articulates the matter, 'doing' consists not of physical action but of sinning, loving, and fearing. She and Anse provide the clearest illustrations, though not the only ones.

Addie's most painful realization has been 'that words are no good; that words don't ever fit what they are trying to say at' (p. 159). 'Motherhood', 'fear', and 'pride' are to her merely words invented by those who have never experienced those emotions, and so is the word 'love' used to her by Anse 'in the nights':

> I knew that that word was like the others: just a shape to fill a lack; that when the right time came, you wouldn't need a word for that any more than for pride or fear (p. 160).

Again the right-angled image is called on to present the total absence of connection between two dimensions of being:

> And so when Cora Tull would tell me I was not a true mother, I would think how words go straight up in a thin line, quick and harmless, and how terribly doing goes along the earth, clinging to it, so that after a while the two lines are too far apart for the same person to straddle from one to the other; and that sin and love and fear are just sounds that people who never sinned nor loved nor feared have for what they never had and cannot have until they forget the words (p. 162).

Anse perfectly exemplifies the meaningless dimension of words. Though a man totally dependent on the exploitation of others, he repeatedly asserts his unwillingness to be beholden to anyone. When he bemoans the effects of the flood ('Eight miles of the sweat of his body washed up outen the Lord's earth, where the Lord Himself told him to put it'—p. 98) and envies town store-keepers 'doing no sweating, living off of them that sweats' (p. 98), it is momentarily possible to forget that Anse never sweats, having persuaded his family that he suffers from a mysterious disease which would kill him if he ever broke into a sweat: Tull observes that

Anse's shirts can be distinguished from those of any other man by the absence of sweat-marks. For Anse, the word 'sweat' is, as Addie would have said, 'just a shape to fill a lack': it serves in place of doing. It is not that he is a hypocrite or a schemer: to be a hypocrite or a schemer implies an awareness of what one is about: Anse simply lives in the dimension of words.

But the dimensions of words and inertia are not one and the same. Cora Tull is ever ready for action, but she, too, lives in words. Addie remarks,

> She prayed for me because she believed I was blind to sin, wanting me to kneel and pray too, because people to whom sin is just a matter of words, to them salvation is just words too (p. 165).

For Addie sin is real and the price of it is paid in doing: 'My daily life is an acknowledgment and expiation of my sin' (p. 154). Cora believes that only God knows what is and what is not sin, and that the duty of the human being is verbal, 'to praise His mercy and His holy name in the hearing of our fellow mortals' (p. 154). She is so blinded by words that she believes Addie's sin was to have failed to respond 'when Brother Whitfield wrestled with her spirit, singled her out, and strove with the vanity in her mortal heart' (p. 154), while to Addie the reality of her sin was her physical response to the preacher, leading to the act of adultery with him, and to the birth of Jewel.

Brother Whitfield, as his relationships with Cora and Addie suggest, is not divided between words and doings, but lives simultaneously in both dimensions like two men, as is recognized by Tull:

> His voice is bigger than him. It's like they are not the same. It's like he is one, and his voice is one, swimming on two horses side by side across the ford and coming into the house, the mud-splashed one and the one that never even got wet, triumphant and sad (p. 83).

It is Whitfield's verbal self that has escaped unsplashed. On his way to the Bundrens' house, he has framed the words in which he will confess his adultery to Anse, but when, on arriving, he finds that Addie has died without revealing their sin, he decides to remain quiet, since once the words have been formulated in his mind it 'was already as though it were done' (p. 167), and the Lord 'will accept the will for the deed' (p. 168). For Whitfield's two selves inhabit different worlds.

In this he is unlike Darl who is torn between words and doing. Darl is essentially a thinker (which is why nearly a third of the monologues are from him) and according to Tull this is what is wrong with him, 'he just thinks by himself too much' (p. 64). It is when his sense of the words uttered by the putrefying body drives him into the action of setting fire to the barn that his already unstable mind begins to split in two, just as Addie had foretold in her distinction between the plane of words and the plane of doing: 'after a while the two lines are too far apart for the same person to straddle from one to the other'. As Darl, betrayed and seized, tells Cash, the 'I' who set fire to the barn is another 'I' (p. 225): the splitting of his psyche is formally represented in his final monologue where he speaks to himself as Darl, in the third person—a separate being with whom he converses but whom he cannot understand.

Darl is equally important in the *rigidity-fluidity* contrast, the right-angled image for which occurs on the first page of the novel, when Jewel and Darl are crossing the field by a path 'straight as a plumb-line', Jewel fifteen feet behind his brother. At the dilapidated cotton-house, the path makes 'four soft right angles' round it, and then continues across the field. Darl, reaching the cotton-house, turns aside to follow the path round it: Jewel, on the other hand, does not deviate:

> looking straight ahead, [he] steps in a single stride through the window. Still staring straight ahead, his pale eyes like wood set into his wooden face, he crosses the floor in four strides with the rigid gravity of a cigar-store Indian dressed in patched overalls and endued with life from the hips down, and steps in a single stride through the opposite window and into the path again just as I come around the corner (pp. 1–2).

He is now five feet ahead of Darl. Throughout the novel, wooden-ness and rigidity are the attributes of Jewel's appearance, as unwavering forward movement characterizes his behaviour. His purpose is undeviating because it follows a straight line without other dimension. He is infuriated by any suggestion of a pause for reflection or any recognition of the smell from the coffin: such things to him are irrelevant. His passion for his mother is intense and regardless of circumstance: it prompts his determination, but once that determination is engaged, he has neither concern nor respect for the body. When the coffin is being borne downhill to the wagon, he is impatient with the care of the other bearers, 'balancing it as though it were something infinitely precious', rushes on impetuously until he alone has it, and 'sloughs it into the wagon-bed' in fury (p. 89). He recovers the coffin from the fire, but as though it were an empty box, toppling it over and over, and crashing out of the barn as though riding it. A rigid fury drives him on, brushing aside anything and anyone that gets in his way, totally single-minded.

Darl, on the other hand, thinks of himself as fluid, and is only too aware that his being is different in kind from his brother's:

> In a strange room you must empty yourself for sleep. And before you are emptied for sleep, what are you. And when you are emptied for sleep, you are not. And when you are filled with sleep, you never were. I don't know what I am. I don't know if I am or not. Jewel knows he is, because he does not know that he does not know whether he is or not. He cannot empty himself for sleep because he is not what he is and he is what he is not (p. 73).

Darl has none of Jewel's passion for his mother. From birth he has been regarded by Addie as a deceit worked on her by Anse under the cover of the word 'love', and he is aware that there is no mother–son relationship between them: 'I cannot love my mother because I have no mother' (p. 86). 'Motherhood' for him, as for Addie, is one of the empty words. For him, inside the coffin there is not an abstracted mother-figure but a dead woman. He is the first to be aware of the smell and of the pursuing buzzards, and the only member of the family to perceive that they are committing an offence against the dignity of the corpse. When they first lift the coffin to load it on the wagon, he imagines it resisting, 'as though within it her pole-thin body clings furiously, even though dead, to a sort of modesty, as she would have tried to conceal a soiled garment that she could not prevent her body soiling' (p. 88); and, finally, at Gillespie's, he hears the putrefying corpse praying to God 'to hide her away from the sight of man' (p. 200). He has no rigid sense of purpose: initially he accepts the plan to transport the coffin to Jefferson; he is engaged in the attempt to cross the flooded river; but his imagination, which flows into the experience of others, flows too into the situation of the corpse, and this leads to disaster. The sympathetic imagination is a weakness, a vulnerability in the plane of action, where what succeeds is the rigid will, untouched by other considerations: it is also regarded as both strange and threatening by other people. Tull observes that it is this which has made Darl talked about:

I always say it ain't never been what he done so much or said or anything so much as how he looks at you. It's like he had got into the inside of you, someway. Like somehow you was looking at yourself and your doings outen his eyes (p. 112).

It is precisely because Dewey Dell is aware that Darl intuitively knows her secret that she hates him, betrays him, and is the first to fling herself on him, 'scratching and clawing at him like a wild cat' after the burial (pp. 224–5). The fluidity of Darl's sympathetic imagination, which enables him to understand others, destroys his sense of self, alienates those whom he penetrates, and places him in a different dimension of being. Because of it he is considered strange and unbalanced and is ultimately isolated in an asylum. He does not (despite some critical suggestions) set himself against Jewel's will: they simply inhabit different worlds. In almost the last sentence of the novel, Cash recognizes the incompatibility of Darl's experience with that of the people around him: 'This world is not his world; this life his life' (p. 248).

The last of the pairs, *space-time*, is plainly dimensional, and the confusion of the two in the novel is ubiquitous and chronic. The journey itself was promised and embarked on because it seemed merely a matter of traversing a comparatively short space, but, from the beginning, the main problem is temporal, the decay of the corpse. When the family sets out, Darl perceives the journey as being through time rather than space:

We go on, with a motion so soporific, so dreamlike as to be uninferant of progress, as though time and not space were decreasing between us and it (p. 96).

This in itself is ominous, because to diminish separating space is the purpose of travel, but diminishing time threatens the fulfilment of that purpose.

The recurrent right-angled image occurs when the family prepare to cross the ford. Looking at the dwarfed figures on the farther shore, Darl thinks,

It is as though the space between us were time: an irrevocable quality. It is as though time, no longer running straight before us in a diminishing line, now runs parallel between us like a looping string, the distance being the doubling accretion of the thread and not the interval between (pp. 133–4).

The fluidity of Darl's nature makes him wish that the self could dissolve into the flow of time:

> If you could just ravel out into time. That would be nice. It would be nice if you could just ravel out into time (p. 196).

The rest of the Bundrens seem incapable of understanding the dimension of time. For Jewel, the transport of the coffin is purely a spatial problem: he neither thinks nor wishes to be reminded of what time is doing to his mother's body. Inability to think in time produces an extraordinary obliviousness to consequences. Cash's broken leg is encased in raw cement in order to hold it still while the movement in space to Jefferson is completed: it occurs to no one, not even Cash, that the price of this temporary immobility of the limb is that he will 'have to limp around on one short leg for the balance of [his] life' (p. 227). Even the mental confusions of the boy Vardaman derive from a confusion of the two dimensions. The famous single-line monologue—'My mother is a fish' (p. 76)—(which, despite symbolic interpretations, still seems to me glib and clever rather than convincing) comes from his inability to distinguish space from time. He had caught a huge fish: it lay in the dust before the house: his mother was then alive. The fish was chopped up: his mother was then dead. Therefore, if the fish were not chopped up but still lay in the dust, his mother would not be dead. He runs to Tull's house to insist that Tull remembers seeing the fish. If Tull will confirm that the fish was there in the dust, it will be as if it were still there and his mother will still be alive. Tull can be taken back to the spot. He can move back in space. Why not, then, in time? It is only Darl in the family who knows that time is 'an irrevocable quality'.

Even when Darl goes crazy and travels by train to the asylum at Jackson, Vardaman can perceive no connection between the events, because causal relationships occur in time. 'Going crazy' is bad, and 'going in a train' is good: he can see no relation between one and the other:

> *He went to Jackson. He went crazy and went to Jackson both. Lots of people didn't go crazy. Pa and Cash and Jewel and Dewey Dell and me didn't go crazy. We never did go crazy. We didn't go to Jackson either* (p. 238).

For Vardaman the two events are linked only by the verb 'went'. He cannot distinguish between the temporal verb of 'went crazy' and the spatial verb of 'went to Jackson'.

The recurring right-angled images, at least one associated with each pair of incompatible dimensions, are not obtrusive and are powerfully effective in their immediate contexts, but they also draw attention to the underlying pattern of the novel—a pattern which, I believe, partly explains the variety of labels affixed by the critics. *As I Lay Dying* is not an epic or a legend, nor merely a tale of a bunch of ignorant and inarticulate hill-farmers engaged in a pointless but obstinately pursued project. It is a novel which very deliberately presents, in the story of some simple people, the welter of incongruent forces and dimensions which make up experience.

The constant interplay of these irreconcilable elements is what justifies or requires Faulkner's otherwise surprising choice of interior monologue. The journey is, of course, structural; it is the basis of the book's narrative and chronology. But the significant action takes place in the experience of those involved in the journey or forced to observe or contribute to it. The climax of the novel is not the burial of Addie—that, in fact, is not witnessed—but the betrayal and madness of Darl, a madness resulting from his inability to continue living in divergent dimensions. They tear him apart, because unlike the rest of his family he cannot shut his mind to them—cannot, like Anse, rest in a world of words and inertia, or, like Jewel, commit himself rigidly and unquestioningly to a course of action, or, like all the others, disregard the dimension of time.

Even the inconsistency of the language of the interior monologues reflects the incongruous forces at work in the characters. Faulkner draws no distinct line between the workings of the conscious and the unconscious minds—though Anse appears to have no unconscious; instead he allows changes of language to suggest the drift from the conscious mind to deeper compulsions and forces. We see beneath the bewildered stammerings of the conscious (as in Dewey Dell's anxieties about her secret or Darl's attempts to consider his own nature) the natural rhetorical images suggestive of the unapprehended energies at work beneath the surface.

The vision of irreconcilable dimensions and forces justifies the remarkable juxtaposition in the novel of the tragic, the comic, the revolting, the absurd, the noble, the degenerate, and all the rest of its strange mixture. Such a vision is essentially ironic: it sees life as a situation from which there is no escape and which humanity can neither comprehend nor cope with, and yet in which it has to live as though it could do both. The more the individual tries to comprehend, the less is he able to cope: the more fully human he is, the more bewildered. In such a life, the animal shrewdness of Anse, never looking far beyond the next moment but seizing any opportunity that occurs, has the best chance of survival. The struggle to overcome human limitations produces tragedy: ignorance of them or failure to recognize them produces comedy or farce. The title of the novel, *As I Lay Dying*, refers essentially not to Addie Bundren's death-bed, but to life as something to be lived through, a process of 'getting ready to stay dead' a long time.

In his emphasis on the novel's simplicity, Faulkner could not have expected to be taken seriously; there is too much evidence of careful planning and complex craftsmanship. Cash has an extraordinary monologue in which he enumerates the principles of the art of making a coffin. He has bevelled all the planks because that gives more surface for the nails and will make the coffin more water-tight: 'Water moves easiest up and down or straight across' (p. 75). Moreover, in a house, where people are upright, stress is up-and-down and seams and joints must be up-and-down; and, in a bed, where people lie down, the stress is sideways, and so the joints and seams are made sideways; but in a coffin the stresses, due to animal magnetism and subsidence of the grave, come slanting 'so the seams and joints of a coffin are made on the bevel':

    12. So I made it on the bevel.
    13. It makes a neater job (p. 75).

The two-fold recurrence of the right-angled diagram in that passage suggests that it may refer not merely to Cash's detached skill in constructing his mother's coffin but also to Faulkner's art and craftsmanship in shaping his novel, taking into account the contrary pressures meeting at the seams and joints of the monologues, so that a slant or bevel is the surface of their interaction. He certainly made a very neat job of it, or, as he put it, 'a simple *tour de force*'.[4]

[4] Frederick L. Gwynn and Joseph L. Blotner (eds.), *Faulkner in the University* (Charlottesville, 1959), p. 87.

Notes on contributors

Beatrice White is Professor Emeritus of the University of London of which she is a graduate. While London has been her intellectual centre, she has enjoyed the privilege of teaching and lecturing in the States and in France and Germany. She was editor of *The Year's Work in English Studies* from 1956 to 1965, and edited three volumes for the *Early English Text Society*. Her interest in history has found expression in her biography of Mary Tudor and her study of the Overbury case, *Cast of Ravens*. Such leisure as retirement affords she devotes to omnivorous reading.

Marie Collins has taught at University College London, Liverpool University, and Westfield College, University of London, where she now lectures. She has published on *Hamlet* and medieval drama, religious literature including *Piers Plowman* and Brigittine didactic prose, the medieval figure of Judas Iscariot, and on legal language and imagery in Chaucer and Gower. She is currently doing further work on Judas Iscariot, and on Brigittine prose in collaboration with Michael Tait.

William Tydeman is currently University Reader in English at the University College of North Wales. His publications include editions of plays by Tom Robertson for C.U.P. and of *Four Tudor Comedies* for Penguin Books; he is also author of *The Theatre in the Middle Ages* (1978), and of a volume on *Dr Faustus* in the Text and Performance series.

J.R. Watson is Professor of English, University of Durham. His recent publications include *Wordsworth's Vital Soul* (Macmillan, 1982) and the anthology *Everyman's Book of Victorian Verse* (Dent, 1982). A volume, *English Poetry of the Romantic Period, 1789–1830*, is in the press. His principal interests are in Romantic and Victorian poetry, especially in landscape and hymnology.

Philip Drew is Emeritus Professor of English at the University of Glasgow. He has published books and articles on a wide range of literary topics, particularly in the Victorian period. He also worked in the field of the history of ideas, where his most recent publication is *The Meaning of Freedom*, an extended study of the treatment in major literary texts of the ideas of fate and free will. In 1983 he delivered a series of lectures on the Gifford foundation under the title *The Literature of Natural Man*.

Dr K.C. Phillipps, Senior Lecturer in English at the University of Leicester, is the author of books on *Jane Austen's English* (1970), *The Language of Thackeray* (1978), *Language and Class in Victorian England* (1984); and also of *Westcountry Words and Ways* (1976). These books represent his main research interests of the English language in the nineteenth century, and the dialect of the South-West.

Charles Peake is Professor of English Literature at Queen Mary College, London University. He is the author of *James Joyce: The Citizen & the Artist* (1977) and edited *Poetry of the Landscape and the Night* (1967) and *Samuel Johnson: 'Rasselas' and Essays* (1967). Most of his published essays and articles deal with the literature of the eighteenth and twentieth centuries.